OPEN HEAVENS

A Study On The Art Of
Intercessory Warfare

Augusto L. Perez

All scripture references are taken from the King James
Version of the Bible.

OPEN HEAVENS
A Study on the Art of Intercessory Warfare
By Augusto L. Perez
ISBN 978-0967847337

All scripture references are taken from the
King James Version of the Bible.

Published by:
Augusto L. Perez

For more information on our ministry or to place an order
please contact us at:

The Appearance Ministries, Inc.
P.O. Box 465
Live Oak, FL. 32064
Web Address: www.theappearance.com
Email: augusto@theappearance.com

DEDICATION

I dedicate this book to the countless, faceless warriors who
gave their lives in the field of battle as martyrs so that
the kingdom of God would prevail, and the glory of
the gospel of Jesus Christ would shine upon the
hearts of thousands of people who otherwise
would never have been able to receive
the wonderful gift of eternal life.

I honor you.

ACKNOWLEDGEMENTS

I want to acknowledge my Father and Lord Jesus Christ whose love for me is so profound that sometimes I am not able to comprehend it, and my precious constant friend and advisor the Holy Spirit, without whom I would not have been able to write this book.
I love you.

I also want to thank so many servants of God, some no longer with us, who inspired and helped me to write this book. Their experience and material were a source of great blessing to me.
Thank you.

TABLE OF CONTENTS

PREFACE

Have you ever wondered why in one city there seems to be open heavens with signs, wonders and miracles taking place, while in another the heavens appear to be made out of brass as if God is withholding His blessing? If we are going to discover the answer to this puzzling question, we must go back to the very foundation of the early Church in America that produced earth shaking revivals and giants of the faith such as Jonathan Edwards, John Wesley, Charles Finney, William Seymour and the early Pentecostal and Healing Movements.

If we have any hope of impacting our cities and changing the course of our nation, we must begin by changing the present day condition of the Church. In its present weakened condition the Church in America will not be able to change itself, let alone impact the cities. A paradigm shift needs to take place in the consciousness of the pastors and their congregations, to shake them out of their slumber and wake up to the reality that we are in the middle of a spiritual war zone.

The Lord wants to send revival to this nation, but it is not going to take place just by the force of confession, or by using a new Madison Avenue or Hollywood fabricated cart and oxen to usher it in. It just will not happen. The Church in America has become a reflection of the society in which it exists, one that feeds on fast (junk) food while watching their favorite TV show, while thinking that a visitation of God can somehow mystically take place somehow, someday.

The present day western mindset is a combination of both anti-supernatural agnosticism and religious mysticism. The early church understood the reality of the supernatural world and lived accordingly. They practiced righteous living and the fear of God. They believed in angels, demons, prayer, fasting and preached conviction messages in the churches. As a result, preachers and believers lived victorious pure lives that glorified and honored the Lord Jesus Christ, and multitudes of people were converted to the kingdom of God.

7

The present religious wineskin (structure) cannot contain the outpouring that is fixing to take place. Many high places are going to have to come down, and major shifts and changes take place in the Church if it wants to be a part of what the Lord is about to do in the world. The Apostolic Reformation that is coming will impact and transform cities and nations as apostolic houses begin to release God's power and authority.

This is not a pipe dream, but the only true foundation upon which the Kingdom of God should be built. Everything else is but shifting sands that cannot withstand the storms that are about to come against the world. Any church that has been built upon any foundation other than the Apostles and Prophets, Jesus Christ Himself being the chief cornerstone (Ephesians 2:20-22), will not be able to survive the great shaking that is about to take place. An Apostolic Reformation is about to take place on this earth that will shake the Church to its very foundation, and prepare the Bride for the soon return of our Lord and Savior Jesus Christ.

An Elijah generation is rising up that will not be afraid of confronting the powers of darkness oppressing our cities and nation. But it starts with each believer getting his own house in order, then the families coming under the authority of the King. The Churches need to get into alignment and begin to function as the Lord ordained it, and then we will be able to take our cities back for God. The Lord is calling His Remnant, a church within a church to rise up and come out from hiding, and take their rightful place in the Body of Christ that God ordained from the foundation of the world.

Come, oh mighty man and woman of God! Let the Lord of Hosts train your hands to war and fingers to fight (Psalms 144:1) the only way we are able to fight this war and win: *Intercessory Warfare.* If you do not have a preaching/teaching ministry, yet you feel that God has called you to intercession, this book will teach you what you need to know about intercessory warfare, and help you to become one of the end-times warrior intercessors that will usher in the great double portion outpouring of His Spirit upon this earth.

INTRODUCTION

It all began in the city of Villanueva, Honduras in January 2007. I had asked all the intercessors of the house to come forth and stand around the altar. The Lord had shown me to anoint the intercessors with oil, lay hands and pray for them. Afterwards, I instructed them to begin to pray and intercede in the spirit and how to do it. The whole thing was orchestrated by the Holy Spirit and everything went flawlessly.

As they began to pray, the power of God filled the house; mighty healings and miracles began to take place as many were saved and delivered that night. However, I felt that there was more, and the Lord did not disappoint me. The following night when the pastor turned the service over to me, I felt that Jesus had not been welcomed properly, so I asked all the people to stand up to their feet and begin to worship the Lord.

Five minutes went by, then ten, then twenty. Suddenly the people started clapping, first a few, then more and more as they kept worshipping the Lord. Twenty five minutes went by, then thirty. I remember thinking upon hearing the sound of two thousand people worshipping God with shouts and clapping, how it compared to the sound of many waters described by the Apostle John in the book of Revelation.

Suddenly I said in Spanish: *"Las lluvias han llegado, las lluvias han llegado!"* announcing the arrival of the outpouring rains as the heavens opened, and an outpouring the likes of which I had never seen started to take place. Large groups of people that were standing started to stagger and fall under the power of the Holy Spirit while another group began to collapse from their chairs as if an invisible hand knocked them over.

Supernatural miracles, healings, deliverances and massive conversions started happening all at the same time, but nobody was praying for them. The Lord was running everything and man had nothing to do with it. It seemed to me at that moment, that anything I would have prayed for, the Lord would have done. The level of faith was so high and the atmosphere so charged with the electric presence of God, that anything would have been possible. We had just experienced open heavens, and I will never forget that moment as long as I live.

The Lord spoke to me and said: *"What you have seen tonight, I also want to do in America; but it will only happen if the intercessors there begin to pray and intercede".* When I came back home, the Lord gave me several visions and dreams all dealing with the coming outpouring rains upon this nation. He again repeated to me that this would only take place if the intercessors would rise up and do much intercessory warfare.

Some time afterwards, the Azusa Street Centennial celebration took place in California with hundreds of thousands in attendance, where there was a heavy emphasis placed on intercessory prayer. Everywhere I went and shared the visions and dreams the Lord had given me about the double portion rains, He confirmed it with signs following. In places where it had not rained for months, rain started to fall by the end of the service. This was repeated several times in many parts of the nation as I shared the word of the Lord.

Since that time, the Lord has commissioned me to raise-up and train intercessors everywhere. We have already conducted Intercessory Prayer Seminars in many different parts of this nation and overseas. The saints are so hungry for this type of material, that many of them started asking me if I had a book available on this subject that they could use as reference for their intercessory prayer ministry. The more I prayed about it, the more I realized that it needed to get done.

We wrote this book in the hope that it will fulfill a great need in the Body of Christ by helping those who feel the call to intercessory warfare. I pray that there will be an impartation as you read the pages of this book, and the eyes of your understanding will be enlightened as the gifts within you are stirred up, activated and put into practice. As you draw closer to God, may you become one of the intercessory prayer warriors He will use in these end-times to create an open heaven over your city, and receive a double portion outpouring of the Holy Spirit (John 1:51).

1

PRAYER LEVEL ONE

"Learning to Pray"

A. THE PRAYER MODEL

On this volume we will be addressing the deeper levels of prayer as it pertains to intercessory prayer and spiritual warfare. If you are a new convert and have never had a prayer life, you might want to first read our book titled: "Foundational Principles for New Converts and Believers", where we dedicate a whole chapter to the prayer model taught by the Lord, and teach you to use it as a blueprint for prayer.

The Lord wanted His disciples to know how to pray and have a life of prayer. Prayer is the one thing that every born again believer should know how to do. Not every believer is called to be in the five-fold ministry and travel the world or pastor a church. However, every single one of us needs to learn how to pray effectively for ourselves, our family, friends and any type of situation that we may encounter in our lives.

While on this earth we go through many trials and wilderness experiences that we need to learn how to overcome. Here is where God begins to train us in prayer, strengthening our faith and establishing our prayer habits, so that when we come to a mountain we can overcome it; or when we face a strong man in our lives we can bind him. Mountains are sent into our lives to stop us from going forward in our walk and ministry, and stop God's blessings from coming into our life.

Jesus came to manifest God's Kingdom on the earth. He wanted to show us what happens when the Kingdom of God is manifested. He wanted to reveal to us that when we move in His Kingdom, it is a spiritual dimension that dominates even the material world. The disciples noticed that when Jesus prayed, the Kingdom of Heaven manifested itself on the earth; so they asked Jesus to teach them how to pray. Jesus gave them a model for prayer that many today use in their prayer life. But to this day, most believers have no clue what it means; and the few who do know what it means, only have a vague understanding of what the Lord was really talking about.

His prayer had as its main focus to exalt the Father, and secondly that the kingdom of heaven and earth would become one. To manifest the Kingdom is not to convince people intellectually leaving the masses of people unconverted, but to manifest the power of God (1 Corinthians 4:19-20). Prayer is broken down into four parts: Worship, petition, penitence and prophetic proclamation. Let us take a look at it in detail.

1.   Praise And Worship

"Our Father who is in heaven, hallowed is your name" God inhabits the praises of His people. David knew that and said it in Psalm 22:3. Praise turns our attention from our problem to God. King Jehoshaphat knew about praise. When he sent the army into battle, he put the singers right in the front lines. He knew the power that was released when the very first people who went out starting praising God. The enemy turned on themselves and killed each other. By the time the army arrived, it was all over. Praise has greater power than any physical force in this world. David also knew its power. He employed musicians and worshippers full time to do that.

a.   Coming into the Throne Room

The first thing you have to do in prayer is to come into the throne room of God. You come into the throne room through praise and worship. The prophet has a unique ability to come into the presence of God because his spirit is in tune with God and can see and hear in the spirit. When you start to praise and worship, you begin to be lifted from this world. You begin to look down at what is happening on the earth from heavenly places. You don't pray from down here. You need to get up there onto the throne with the Lord, because we are with Him and He is in you. And if we are seated with Him in heavenly places, spiritually we are seated on the throne. You need to get your eyes off this physical plane and be lifted up so you can now look down. We pray from heavenly places. Worship and praise Him and stay in His presence waiting for Him to give you something and then release it in the earth.

b. Prophetic Intercessor

Prophetic and intercessor are synonymous because intercession is the main function of a prophet. It is not to predict and speak nice words of personal prophecy over people and tell them what their future is and who they will marry or whether they will be rich. Psychics do that. This is not the work of the prophetic ministry. The work of the prophetic ministry is to release the will of God into the earth. In order to do that, we need to start by coming into the throne room. From there you do warfare and intercession. But you won't get there except by starting in praise and worship. That is why praise and worship is the first instruction in prayer.

A prophet has the ability to bring the anointing presence of God into a meeting because he has the ability to move into the throne room very quickly. And when you move into the throne room, you begin to communicate down here while your spirit is up there, and you begin to communicate the very presence of God outwards into the place that you are.

c. Music

Prophets usually use music and singing to release the power of God. It does not matter if you cannot sing well, or if you have no musical abilities. Start by singing in tongues, going up and down the scales. You are creating harmony in spirit, soul and body which releases God's anointing power.

Music has the ability to bring resonance to the soul. Music is the only thing that has the ability to take your mind, emotions and will and cause them to flow together in harmony at the same time, in tune with your spirit. Your whole spirit, soul and body begin to vibrate with the very power of God. His glory begins to come upon you and radiate forth through you as you start moving into that. So the prophet enters the presence of God thru praise and worship. Once you come into the Throne Room, then you begin to wage warfare in the Spirit.

2.   Petition

This is the prayer most people know. When Christians pray, they need to know if they had their prayers answered or not (I John 5:14). In order for prayer to be effective, it has to be done according God's word and God's will.

a.   Praying According to God's Word

The word of God is the plumb line to which everything must line up to. It is like the railroad tracks upon which the locomotive of our prayer life and Christian walk must travel on. No matter how good something sounds, if it goes against the word of God, throw it away.

Whatever you pray for, make sure your prayer lines up with the word of God. That is why it is so important to hide the word of God in your heart, so that whenever you are in prayer or during a time of need you can pray the word of God.

Remember key passages of scriptures that have to do with promises of God regarding salvation, provision, deliverance, protection, healing and so forth. These will come in handy when you are going through trials and times of testing in your own life, or when you are praying for a loved one or a friend.

God's Word is general and may not apply to the situation you or someone else may be going through at the moment, which brings us to the topic of God's will.

b. Praying According to God's Will

The will of God takes into account the very desires of your heart as He never imposes anything on us. He knows what we are capable of; our talents, abilities, experiences and according to these things the Lord makes a plan according to your prayer. God will never overrule your will.

To pray according to God's will, means to pray according to what God wants to accomplish on the earth in a certain circumstance. When we pray and wait on the Lord, He has taken what we have given Him and has designed a plan for us, and all we need to do is get in line with that plan and let it run its course. If we miss the perfect plan He laid out for us, we may have to start all over again with God's plan B.

It's just like when you miss an exit in the expressway. You may be able to get off on the next exit, but by the time you arrive there, your chance has gone and the circumstances have changed. People that were there are not there anymore; the situations that existed, do not exist anymore. They are gone.

Can you imagine what would have happened if Elijah the prophet would have gone to the widow of Zarephath at a different time that the Lord told him to go? The widow would not have been in the field gathering sticks; Elijah would have gone hungry for several days; there would have been no miracle of the barrel of meal and the cruse of oil, and there would have been no resurrection of the widow's son.

That is why we need to have a prayer closet where we meet with Him daily, and be tuned in so we are able to hear His voice, and know God's will in any given situation so we can obey Him and do that which He is showing us.

This is what the prophet does when he decrees things over people, churches and cities. He knows now is the time, the moment for this to be fulfilled. That is why you have to be in tune with the Spirit of God, and be able to hear His voice, walk in obedience and get His perfect timing.

c.   Praying With Faith

Prayer must be done in faith (Mark 11:24). If you do not believe it will not happen. Faith is always past tense. Faith says "God has provided my needs"; "God has healed me"; "It is done, it is mine, it is finished". God answers our prayer of faith through somebody else most of the time. This is where a lot of people get it wrong. If you need healing, he sends you somebody with the gift of healing. If you need direction, He sends you somebody with a word from the Lord. If you need finances or something, he will move on someone to give you what you need.

The Lord always does things on the earth through people. He does nothing until somebody prays. God does nothing except through human agency. It is whatever we bind on earth that is bound in heaven, and whatever we loose on earth is loosed in heaven. This is what the ministry of prophetic intercession is all about. The prophetic decree has the authority to release into the atmosphere the rhema word of God that has been revealed, releasing on the earth the authority for the answer to your prayer of faith to take place.

d.   Praying For Another

This is how the Lord starts to train you to pray for your family and friends in a very low level of intercession. This type of prayer is a friend, praying to a friend for a friend. This is how God begins to train us in the art of intercessory prayer. The Lord teaches us to be persistent and persevere in prayer until we pray through and receive an answer. We learn how to *ask, seek and knock.*

It is during this time that God develops our faith, teaching us the value of perseverance and patience in obtaining the things we are asking Him for. He teaches us how to pray according to His will, not ours. Here we learn how to manifest His Kingdom on the earth, and discover His will for us on this earth. Not only do we learn to discover His will for us individually, but also His will for specific situations and other people in our lives as well. It takes some time to be able to develop and master this level of prayer life as we mature as Christians and grow in the faith.

If the Lord is showing you something, do not start just to pray for it, but wait until the Lord shows you how to pray. Maybe you will only speak protection and blessing on someone. Perhaps you will stand in the gap and repent for someone, or you may release the will of the Lord on them through a decree or you will go into warfare on behalf of them.

Wait to see what the Lord really wants to do. Do not push through it impatiently, but pray and stay with it until you are through and feel a peace in your spirit about it. Do not give up before it's time. You will feel it, and know when it is time to stop. You need to let the Holy Spirit lead you.

Intercessory prayer is exciting and awesome, but it is hard work. It is more than just praying for another person's needs. It sometimes may mean not only praying for another person, but praying as another person. How can you fully pray on behalf of another without fully understanding their given situation and what is on their heart?

The Lord sometimes gives the intercessor the ability to enter into the spirit and feel, know and experience the very conflict and agony that person is going through. The intercessor will sometimes experience the same pain and anguish in the body of that other person. The intercessor will begin to groan, wail, travail and feel despair.

This can be very confusing if you don't know what is taking place. What is happening to you as an intercessor is that you have literally become that person in the spirit, and are praying as that person in the spirit, petitioning God on behalf of that person. Jesus is the greatest intercessor ever. He is praying for you. Every time you sin, He intercedes for you.

3. Repentance

When we sin, we come under condemnation because our heart condemns us. If our heart condemns us, then we will not have confidence towards God. We come under condemnation. Repentance clears our pipes if you will, because it clears our hearts and helps us to pray with confidence (1 John 3:21).

a. Repenting on Behalf of Others

This is a principle that has taken place throughout the Bible. Daniel interceded and confessed the sins of a whole nation. An intercessor often will receive the burden and guilt of sin as they are interceding on behalf of somebody else, and take on the burden to the Lord in prayer. We have the power to speak forgiveness to God's people. At the end of the gospel of John Jesus came to His disciples, breathed on them and said, *"Receive the Holy Spirit"* and then said to them: *"Whosoever sins you remit, they are remitted, and the sins you retain, they are retained."*

There is a release and healing when you hear someone else saying to you that your sins are forgiven. It has the power to set people free from guilt and condemnation. There are certain sins unto death that John tells us not to pray for (I John 5:16). There are sins that bring curses upon people's lives and come directly against the kingdom of God.

b. Breaking Curses over Other People

There are many different kinds of sins. There are sins that people are caught in; sins affecting people because they are under a generational curse; sins that bring people under the curse of others they may be associated with, or those who have spoken negative words over them. An intercessor has the authority to intercede on behalf of other people and break the curses over them. He has the authority to break the power of sin over their lives and speak life to them.

You may set people free from bondages that are binding them by speaking in the Spirit: *"In the name of Jesus, I speak forgiveness, cleansing to you now and I set you free from all bondages."* The power will be broken. This is a very powerful type of prayer that is not done often, but is part of the ministry that should be ministered to God's people.

4.   The Prophetic Decree

Let us take a look at the part of the prayer model that says: *"Thy kingdom come, your will be done on earth as it is in heaven"*. We need to take a look at the original Greek text to understand it properly. *"Thy kingdom come, your will be done on the earth as it is in heaven"* is an imperative command. The will of God is released on this earth through words and actions. So when you pray, you release it on this earth and it will cause something. If you do not pray in the will of God, you can bind people and make it worse instead of blessing them.

This is a powerful and essential part of intercession. When we are interceding from the throne room of God, we are issuing decrees from the throne. We are not praying up to the throne, but praying down from there. When you stand in that place as God's spokesman on the earth, you can issue a divine decree, a commandment. As an example, we can take a look at the decree of some kings made in the Old Testament. King Balthazar did it in regard to Daniel and the lion's den; King Ahasuerus did it in the book of Esther. They both made decrees that could not be brought back.

Once a divine decree is issued, it cannot be retracted because whatever God speaks becomes law, and even God is submitted to His own word. When the word of God goes out of His mouth, it will hit the target every time (Isaiah 55:11). You cannot put a bullet back into the mouth of a rifle once you have fired it. When any believer, but especially a prophet of God, opens his mouth to speak forth the word that the Lord has placed in his heart, a decree is sent forth into the earth that cannot be retracted (Amos 3:7).

That is why there is a tremendous responsibility in a prophetic intercessor. When an intercessor opens his mouth to decree the authority and the word of God, He must ensure that they are sent to the right place, at the right time and in the proper way. God cannot intervene on the earth without the permission of a human being because it is illegal. This means that when God plans to do something on the earth, He looks for a person he knows and trusts to be His agent because of the law of permission. The Lord depends on human beings to give Him permission to do His will on the earth.

5.   The Ways of God

Many people think that intercession is taking a whole list of requests and hammer it into the kingdom of heaven, and hopefully one of us will get it right and get it answered. But the prayer that gets results is when the intercessor first comes into the presence of God, and right into the throne room.

Once there, he waits for a divine decree. The Lord may tell you to drop it; He may not want to deal with that one. As you are praying, somebody comes into your mind unbidden in a strong way and the Spirit says: *"Speak it forth; pray for that person; I'm going to work in that situation"*. That is when you issue the decree. Intercessors should go to the Lord not as much with a prayer list, as to receive a prayer list from Him. Write down the things He tells you. We can all pray, but the prophet is called specifically to do this. Most true intercessors are really prophets in training.

Intercessory prayer is the main function of the prophetic call. When a true prophet prophesies over an individual, church, city or nation he is speaking the very will of God over them. When this happens, doors are unlocked for them and things happen in the spiritual realm. Apostles and prophets have the authority to bind and loose, open and shut.

All believers have that ability in some way, but apostles and prophets have been given the authority to issue the decree to open the way or shut the door. This is what should be happening and this is done through the ministry of intercession. They are almost synonymous and go together. If you are an intercessor, God is leading you into the prophetic ministry; and if you are a prophetic person, then you are an intercessor.

2

PRAYER LEVEL TWO

"The Legal Battle"

A. UNDERSTANDING THE LEGAL BATTLE

This level of prayer takes us fully into the realm of intercessory prayer where we learn the principles of winning the legal battle over our adversary the devil. Many people ask this valid question: "If Jesus overcame the devil and the powers of darkness at the cross, why do we have to do battle?"(Col. 2:14; Ephesians 6:12)

In order to understand this you need to understand that everything that God does on this earth He does through a human vessel. Angels cannot fight until we get involved in the battle. It is man who enforces the decrees of heaven.

A believer has to go to the heavenly court in prayer and state his case like the widow of Luke 18:3-8, and accuse the devil of illegally trespassing and touching what belongs to you. That is why the Bible says that Jesus is our high priest, making intercession for us in heaven (Romans 8:34).

The Christian who does this must not be living in sin, but be walking a pure walk with God, have a strong faith and trust in the Lord and have perseverance and persistence. One person is enough to enter Heaven's Court.

That believer must then accuse the devil with perseverance and faith without giving up and win the legal battle: *"Lord this is my cause; I take what is mine, my inheritance, and my blessings. I accuse the devil in the name of Jesus. I bind the strong man in my life"*.

Once this legal battle is won and Father gives the verdict in our favor, we then have Heaven's legal permission to enter into spiritual warfare. Now we have permission to enter into the next level of intercessory prayer where angelic beings get activated and involved in warfare to bring down principalities and powers and give us the victory.

B. THE NEED TO PRAY FOR THE LOST

The primary purpose in praying for the lost is not to convince God to save them for He is not willing that any should perish (II Peter 3:9), having sent Christ to die for the sins of the whole world (I John 2:2). But rather it has to do with spiritual warfare, freeing them of demonic influence so they can be saved (Isaiah 14:17; Acts 26:18; 1 John 5:19; Ephesians 2:2).

The apostle Paul stated in the Bible that people who do not know the Lord are blinded by the devil and cannot see the light of the gospel on their own (2 Cor. 4:3-4). Therefore, they cannot be saved unless someone prays for them and frees them from the demonic influences that control them; because they are under the authority of Satan (Eze. 22:30; Acts 26:18).

The scripture says that the devil and the powers of darkness specifically try to keep the people from understanding the gospel (2 Tim. 2:25-26). People can be lulled to sleep by songs of Jesus and watered down preaching because they have never been impacted by the power of the gospel of Jesus Christ. Only when the power of the Holy Spirit is present, can people's ears be opened to receive the saving gospel. A person may hear the gospel hundreds of times, but because they are blind spiritually they are unable to receive it. Preaching the gospel to those whom no one has prayed for is like asking a blind man to see the beauty of nature.

Demonic blindfolds cause the gospel to appear foolish to people. The strong man causes this negative view toward the gospel. Sometimes if you try to share the gospel with someone in this condition may do more harm than good. Unless we first bind the strong man, any attempts we make to spoil his goods will only enrage him and make him strengthen his armor and guard his palace more fiercely (Mark 3:27). When the Holy

Spirit calls you to pray, it is very important that you pray immediately. It may require you to leave a crowded room, cancel some important appointments or even leave your dinner sitting on the table. You must be obedient, which is better than sacrifice. God is not unreasonable, He knows your duties; but many times the things we think are important are not important at all. Our prayer for someone may be what keeps him from going to hell. Therefore, it behooves all of us to learn how to pray effectively for the lost. There are several factors that are absolutely necessary for effective prayer.

C.   PRAYING FOR THE LOST

Because we are kings and priests (1 Peter 2:5; 1 Timothy 2:1-4), our primary responsibility is to first talk to God about men, and then talk to men about God. Procrastination is our greatest enemy. When you look down the road, not doing those things that you considered important will not matter, but it will matter if you prayed. It is not an easy thing to pray intercessory prayers without the help of the Holy Spirit. It is only possible as the Holy Spirit takes over and prays through us. In order to pray effectively for the lost, there are some things we must do.

1.   Pray In Faith

This is an unbreakable law in the kingdom of God. It is always according to your faith. Unbelief is often the cause of unanswered prayer (Mathew 9:29). If you do not have strong faith in what you are asking for, chances are you will not receive an answer to your prayers.

Without faith it is virtually impossible to please God (Hebrews 11). Faith has substance and it is tangible, whether you see it or not. Faith is the only thing that works in the kingdom of God. It is the spiritual currency whereby we have access to the vast supply of blessings and riches in His kingdom. He delights to see faith in his children. Jesus never was impressed with how much people knew, or how many laws they were able to keep, but He was always impressed whenever He saw faith in people (Mathew 8:10; 15:28). Faith and love always work together (Galatians 5:6). Love casts out fear which is like green kryptonite to faith (1 John 4:18).

2.   Pray In Righteousness

The imputed righteousness of Christ which comes through his shed blood is what gives us boldness to approach His throne of grace; but personal righteousness is also crucial (Psalms 66:18; John 15:7). If you have sin reigning in your life, it will give the devil a legal right to object to your prayers and present a case against you in the spiritual court of law.

We must have a pure walk before the Lord. Whenever we commit a sin, we need to repent and confess the sin quickly to the Lord, and the blood of Jesus Christ will wash us from all sin and cleanse us from all unrighteousness (1 John1:9)

3.   Pray in Brokenness

God only answers desperate and passionate prayers. Jesus wept over Jerusalem. Tears are very powerful and God promises a harvest when we do it (Psalm 126:5-6). This is a law of spiritual harvest. Today, however, we want the harvest without the heartbreak. Leonard Ravenhill once said that God usually answers desperate prayer. Until we get desperate for souls, our prayers for them may remain unanswered. Just like Jesus wept over Jerusalem, we must weep over our lost ones if we really want to see them saved. General Booth of the Salvation Army was once asked by one his people what he should do to save the lost. He answered: *"Try tears"*.

As we get close to God in prayer, we will feel His heartbeat and our heart will be broken with the things that break the heart of God. To be able to pray with brokenness we must be able to see ourselves as God sees us. When we repent for our sins and hardness of hearts, we will be able to pray in humility. By humbling ourselves we get in the spirit, where we find it easy to pray even for your enemies. That is why persecuted Christians can pray for their tormentors and those who torture them. You can only do this in the spirit.

4. Travail

Travail is defined in Strong's Dictionary: *"to writhe in pain"*. The process of child birth again illustrates this very well. Just like a mother experiences labor pains in giving physical birth to her baby, the same is true in the spiritual realm. For every person that is born again, someone has interceded and travailed for them (Isaiah 66:8; Romans 8:26-27; Galatians 4:19). Most Christians today do not even pray for the lost, let alone travail. No wonder so few people are being won to the Lord in this nation.

Intercession and travail is very different from normal devotional prayer. You can pray that kind of prayer at any moment, but not travailing prayer. Intercessory prayer is imparted by the Lord and is the kind of prayer that comes with a burden. This is a feeling of sadness, concern, even anxiety. You may or may not know for who the burden is.

Sometimes the Lord may bring the face of the person or name to mind. Immediately you may feel unusual sympathy or concern for the individual. This is how God calls us to pray. But unless you take time to give yourself to intercession, you will not experience *"parturition"*, the actual joy and relief that comes with having given birth to the will of God and having *"prayed through"* (Isaiah 66:8).

When you intercede for people like this, you may experience excruciating agony and pain like in childbirth, actually feeling a person's grief, pain and loneliness. When the Lord places a burden on you to pray it is called: *"The burden of the Lord"*. This is a supernatural experience where God is allowing us to feel His burden, sadness, love and grief. You become pregnant with a burden that is given by the Lord and you travail or groan in delivery until it is accomplished.

Travailing prayer is unpleasant and should be done as much as possible in private. If you are in a meeting and begin to feel a burden to intercede, if possible without causing a disturbance and affecting the service, quietly slip out of the service into a place where your travail will not disturb others. However, if the spirit of intercession supernaturally starts coming upon many people at the same time, it could be directly related to something of great importance that the Lord wants to birth during the service.

The pastor or spiritual leader of the house needs to be sensitive and discerning, being careful not to quench the Holy Spirit. Discernment must be exercised as to how to proceed in the flow of the service. Most pastors and Christian believers in America are not familiar with intercessory prayer, and may not be able to recognize it whenever it manifests in a service.

Remember that the Holy Spirit will only intercede through those who are both willing and obedient. If you are, simply tell the Lord you are both available and willing. Then as you start to feel deep within an intercessory burden begin to stir, come apart and allow the Holy Spirit to move upon you until that for which you are burdened is birthed. Lack of travail is the reason why we do not see results in winning the lost to Christ.

5.   Pray Through

This is an expression that has become obsolete today, but one that was much used by old timers at one time. It means praying until you know in your spirit that your prayer has been answered. Sometimes answers to prayers may take years to come to pass and some you may never see. But as far as heaven is concerned, it is a done deal. The Bible refers to the lost as prisoners that Satan refuses to release because they are under his jurisdiction (Isaiah 14:17; Acts 26:18).

Persistence in prayer is an absolute necessity. The devil has blinded the eyes of the lost and he is not going to let them go that easy. Satan controls entire cities, cultures and countries. One of the devil's favorite tactics is to make the situation look so impossible that we get discouraged and quit praying. The reason he does this is because he really has no defense against prayer. All prayer is warfare, and every time you pray you are causing damage to him, although you may not see any change in your present circumstances. If we could see what happens in the spirit realm when we pray, we would be very encouraged (2 Kings 6:17). You need to keep praying whether you see results or not, because your prayers do have an effect.

6. Pray Aggressively

Praying aggressively is important in intercession because prayer is warfare (2 Corinthians 10:4). The Lord has given us authority on this earth and we need to learn how to exercise it in winning the lost to Christ. We are called to be more than conquerors (Romans 8:37). The people of God must learn how to conduct spiritual warfare and storm the gates of hell, because Satan will not give up the captives without a fight.

The church is in a state of indifference and apathy. Christians languish in lethargy and unbelief, while the devil continues to imprison our loved ones. If believers realized the power God has given them through Christ Jesus, they would start to act differently (Ephesians 1:17-23; 6:10-18). The devil will not surrender any person or territory until it is forcibly wrested from him (Mathew 11:12).

7. Pray With the Right Motive

Our primary motive must be one of love, compassion and obedience. Our motivation must not be rooted in selfishness or pride. If our motives are not pure, we may not get answers to our prayers (James 4:3). In the legal court of law, the opposing attorney can object to a particular argument or certain evidence he believes to be outside the bounds of legality. If the judge agrees, he will then sustain the objection which renders the argument void.

In the spiritual legal battle it is the same. We can pray very eloquently and quote all the right scriptures and biblical reasons, but if our motive is wrong, Satan will object and the Judge may just agree with him rendering all our prayers and pleadings null and void. Remember the devil is a legal expert, and he has thousands of years of experience.

We must learn to pray unselfish prayers. Moses fasted and prayed for the sins of the people of Israel (Deut. 9: 8-19). We also can learn from the example of Esther (Esther 4:16). A true intercessor must learn to lay down his live as a living sacrifice at the altar of God so that others may live, and His Kingdom may be advanced (Romans 12:1).

8. Pray in Unity

Just as a magnifying glass can ignite a fire by capturing the sunlight and concentrating it on one specific spot, likewise when we pray united prayers, it can rout the strong man and focus the power of the spirit on one place (Deuteronomy 32:30; Mathew 18:19). God places an incredible value in unity among His people. Because unity and intercession are rare, when you put these two together you truly have something very rare.

God commands a blessing where there is unity among His people (Psalm 133). There is usually only one strong man controlling the life of a person. Whenever several intercessors come together against the strong man, he is able to be defeated (I John 4:3-4; Luke 11:21-22). Once he is defeated, spoiling his goods becomes a much easier matter.

D. WAGING THE LEGAL BATTLE

Before we are able to wage war against the powers of darkness, we must wage and win the legal battle against the devil by producing an effective case against him (Isaiah 41:21). We have already stated in this chapter that when you start pleading your case before the Lord, you must do so with righteousness, faith and persistence. You need to be able to understand that Satan will present his case against you as well (Job 1:9-11). If your house is not in order, he will be quick to point that out in order to punch holes in your case against him.

Pleading your case before the Lord is nothing new. It has existed for thousands of years. This is what many old timers used to call pleading, and they did it very effectively. Pleading is simply arguing your case before the Lord. A couple of good examples in the Bible are when Abraham pleaded with God so that He would not destroy the cities of Sodom and Gomorrah (Genesis 18) and when Moses pleaded for the lives of the people of Israel (Exodus 32).

Whenever we plead and argue a case before God, we are proving to Him that by His own word, oath and character He has bound Himself. Oaths are very important to the Lord, and He has given us the right to ask and claim those promises.

Once we demonstrate that He has promised it, He will answer us because He cannot deny Himself. Charles Spurgeon once said that *"pleading is the very marrow of prayer"*. There are several things we can plead when waging a legal battle.

1. The Purposes of God for Man

God has a purpose for each person on this earth, and we can use this as an argument when pleading with the Lord about a loved one, or for personal circumstances in your own life (Jeremiah 1:5; Luke 19:10; Acts 26:18; Ephesians 2:5-7).

2. The Promises of God Concerning Salvation

There are many scriptures that reveal to us the heart of God and the way He feels towards those who are lost and helpless (John 3:16; John 6:37). We know from scripture that it is the will of God to save the lost. Whenever you pray for the salvation of a human being, you are praying according to His will, and He will hear and answer you (1 John 5:15).

3. The Power of God

We all have seen the power of God manifested at one time or another in our own lives. We know that God is all powerful, and that He has used that power in the past on behalf of His children numerous times throughout the Bible (Romans 1:16). You can draw from Biblical examples and your own personal experiences to argue your case before the Lord.

4. The Attributes of God

The Lord has many attributes which are part of His nature and character. We learn from scriptures that God does not change, and that He is the same yesterday, today and forever (Malachi 3:6; Hebrews 13:8). You may intercede before Him by reminding Him of His longsuffering, compassion, mercy, love and grace.

E. THE WEAPONS OF OUR WARFARE

Just like all physical weapons of war are used to defeat the enemy, likewise our spiritual weapons are used to do the same (2 Corinthians 10:4-5). These weapons are designed to pull down strongholds and mindsets that go against the word and the will of God. The battle field is a person's mind, because we are dealing with paradigms, traditions, habits and thoughts.

Whoever controls the mind controls the person. That is how Satan controls individuals, and keeps them from being saved. The only way for him to do this is to keep people blinded to the gospel. No person in his right mind would choose Satan over Jesus and hell over heaven. The purpose of prayer is to free the will of men, to rip the veil from their eyes so they can see and receive the gospel of salvation.

Satan uses strongholds like unbelief, greed, lust, drugs, alcohol, homosexuality, rejection, abuse, bitterness, and low self esteem to keep people from coming to the Lord. There is usually one key stronghold in the life of most people that hinders them from receiving the gospel of Jesus Christ.

The battle is always fought over one stronghold that is usually the armor behind which the enemy hides. When his armor or stronghold is destroyed, the person is freed and is ready for salvation. You need to get familiar with all your weapons of warfare that need to be used while you pray.

1. The Blood of Jesus Christ

The devil has absolutely no right upon anyone or anything. Legally all souls belong to Christ because He paid for them on

Calvary (1 John 2:2). It means that all the power the devil has is by deception and bluff. When we plead the blood of Jesus, we remind Satan and all demons that they are defeated (Revelation 12:11; Hebrews 2:14). This is true especially in the battle for souls, since the devil holds them captive only by default, because we have never insisted the he turn them loose.

2.   The Name of Jesus

There are various reasons why the name of Jesus is so powerful in the spiritual realm (Luke 10:17). He is the creator of all things (Colossians 1:16). He overcame death, hell and the grave through His death and resurrection (Revelation 1:18). All power has been given to Him in the heaven and the earth (Mathew 28:18; Philippians 2:9-11). When we intercede for the lost demanding that they be set free, demons must obey because they are subject to His name.

3.   The Word of God

It is no wonder the word of God is called the sword of the Spirit. (Ephesians 6:17). Since Satan was totally stripped of his power and authority at Calvary (Colossians 2:15), all he has to work with is lies, smoke and mirrors. He is able to deceive the whole world (Revelation 12:9). The word of God is truth and light; darkness does not stand a chance.

4.   Worship and Praise

Most people have no idea how powerful praise and worship are in spiritual warfare (Psalm 22:3). Every one who is warrior and intercessor needs to become a true worshipper of the Lord Jesus Christ to replenish their spirit man. Praise and thank God beforehand for what He is going to do in the future.

5.   Fasting

Fasting enhances the power of prayer, and is one of the most potent weapons of warfare we have at our disposal to defeat the enemy (Isaiah 58:6). Some evil spirits can only be defeated by prayer and fasting (Mark 9:29).

6. Love

Those that love the Lord with all their hearts, and have compassion for lost souls cannot be stopped (1 Corinthians 13:7-8; Revelation 12:11). Love cannot fail. Love will succeed where most other things will fail. Do whatever it takes to keep somebody out of hell.

7. Authority in Christ

When we exercise our authority in Him, demons cannot withstand us. God has called us to be instruments through which He can exercise His kingdom authority based on the finished work of the cross (Mathew 16:19). When you accept this position by faith, He will use you in ways that you have never even dreamed of.

No one should die and go to hell because Christ has already paid their redemption price. Satan illegally and forcefully continues to hold human beings captive in spiritual darkness. The devil will not release them until we take our rightful place and exercise our throne rights demanding their immediate release on the basis of the shed blood of Christ and our delegated authority over him. You need to understand that the devil is not going to release them until you make him.

8. Resisting the Devil

When we do intercessory warfare, Satan uses difficult circumstances in life to try to make us quit (Ephesians 6:10-18; James 4:7). That is why the person you are praying for will get worse at first, instead of better. The devil wants you to quit praying because he is loosing his grip on those souls.

Resist him by not allowing negative reactions and circumstances to stop your prayers. No matter what he does, just keep on praying. Satan cannot continue to hold out for long against bold, fervent warfare prayer; eventually he will have to let go (Luke 11:5-13; 18:1-8).

3

PRAYER LEVEL THREE

"Birthing and Intercession"

A. THE PROCESS OF BIRTHING IN CREATION

There is a powerful principle involved in the story of creation in the book of Genesis. Throughout the Bible we are taught this same principle in various, diverse ways and circumstances in the lives of God's people. This is a principle that teaches a believer to appropriate the supernatural power of God's Spirit to create life out of that which is formerly dead and barren. We see in Genesis chapter one that creation was accomplished in a series of steps as God gave form to an empty and formless mass, and filled the earth with living beings.

1. The Spirit Of God Moved Upon The Waters

In the second verse we read that the Spirit of God moved upon the waters. Creation was in its embryonic stage as the earth was *without form* and *void*, not in a very pleasant condition. The Hebrew root word for '*without form*' is *tohuw* which means: *chaos, empty, waste and confusion*. The Hebrew root word for '*void*' is *bohuw* which means: *empty and in ruin*.

In the same second verse, it says that '*darkness'* (*choshek*) was upon the phase of the deep. The Hebrew root word '*choshek'* means: *destruction, death, ignorance, darkness, misery, sorrow, shapeless, useless and wickedness*. Darkness was dispelled as God spoke for there to be light. There can be no life without light. God, who is light, brought life to that which was dead, barren, in darkness and without life.

We continue to read in the second verse that the Spirit of God '*moved'* (*rachaph*) upon the waters. The Hebrew root word *rachaph* means: *move, to brood over as a mother hen broods over her eggs, to breed, to give birth to, reproduce and fertilize*. God was bringing forth life in the physical realm by hovering and brooding over the earth. When we take a deeper, closer look at the spiritual significance of this verse, we start to see how it compares the creation in Genesis to a birthing, where God birthed the world into existence through travail.

We see the same principle when we take a look at the Hebrew root words used in Psalms 90:2: "Before the mountains were '*brought forth*' (*yalad-to travail, to birth, to act as a midwife*), or ever you had '*formed*' (*chuwl-to writhe in pain as in parturition, to grieve, to wait patiently in sorrow, to travail in pain, to bring forth*) the earth and the world, even from everlasting to everlasting, you are God".

We see it again in Isaiah 66:8-9: Who has heard such a thing? Who has seen such things? Shall the earth be made to '*bring forth*' *(chuwl)* in one day? Or shall a nation be '*born*' (*yalad*) at once? For as soon as Zion '*travailed*' *(chuwl)*, she '*brought forth*' *(Yalad)* her children. Shall I bring to the birth, and not cause to '*bring forth*' (*yalad*)? Says the Lord: shall I cause to '*bring forth*' (*yalad*) and shut the womb? Says God.

You are always going to find travail behind every birthing. Mothers understand from personal experience that this is true. The result of travail is that something supernatural occurs as God's power is manifested. As we learn to incorporate travail into our prayers, we will supernaturally bring about life to dead and lifeless situations, people, churches and cities.

2. The Birth Of Jesus And Other Examples

In the New Testament in Luke 1:35, we find the same concept in Mary's conception of Jesus Christ. The Greek word for '*overshadow*' *(episkiazo)* is the counterpart of the Hebrew word for '*hover*' *(rachaph)*. The creative energy of God was released over Mary. The birth of Isaac to Abraham and Sarah was also the result of a supernatural visitation from God's power to Sarah's womb which was dead and barren, as God hovered over Abraham and Sarah until Sarah conceived. God was not only birthing a son, but also a nation.

In the story of the transfiguration in Mathew 17:5, we read that a cloud *'overshadowed'* (*episkiazo*) Jesus Christ on the mountain. That same word is used when the shadow of Peter passed by and *'overshadowed'* and healed the sick in Acts 5:15. Elijah stretched himself over the dead child in 2 Kings 4:32-35 and he came back to life. Jesus Christ wanted to gather His people as a chicken gathers her chicks under her wings and hovers over them (Mathew 23:37). We see the same principle when the eagle stirs up her nest and flutters over her young (Deuteronomy 32:11).

3.   Present Day Conditions

Today we could say that as a result of man's sin, the earth is in a similar condition as in Genesis 1:1-2. God is not only the author of Creation, but also the fountain of life and energy. Dead things will continue to be dead unless God energizes it with His Spirit. The same power that in the beginning brought the world into existence out of darkness, emptiness and confusion, can also restore to us the years the locust has eaten. This is a great hope for all of us.

The Church today is being called to enter into intercession and travail in order to bring our cities and nation from barrenness and lifelessness to life. The power and energy of the Holy Spirit can be released through the birthing process to manifest life on the earth. God has given this privilege to humanity, His most cherished creation, to partake in the birthing process even as He did in the original creation. As intercessors push in travailing prayer, a release will take place in the spiritual realm, birthing new things that will glorify God.

B.   TYPES OF INTERCESSORY PRAYER

Intercessory prayer is the key to unlocking cities and nations by breaking the iron bars that hold the people captive, ripping the veils from their eyes. Some intercessors pray five hours a day or more. When Daniel prayed in Daniel 9, he moved the heavenlies and repositioned the demonic forces as well as angelic beings. He began to release men like Ezra, Nehemiah and prophetic voices for the construction of the city of Jerusalem. This is the kind of prayer needed in this hour to stop the plundering of our cities by demonic forces.

God is raising up intercessors young and old, male and female to do all night prayer meetings, and prayer walks. We are in great need of intercessors. Intercessory prayer has displaced demonic powers in areas like North Korea, China, Argentina, Nigeria, Guatemala and the result is open heavens where churches have grown by the thousands. This kind of intercessory prayer is not passive, but aggressive and confrontational. It names principalities and powers by name and brings them down.

These intercessors pray many hours a day. This produces tremendous power in the Holy Spirit in the form of healings, miracles, signs and wonders. We need to begin to release within us intercessory prayer so that angels of God will intervene and wage battle in the heavenlies. Now let us take a look at some types of intercessory prayer:

1.   Birthing

This is probably the most well known type of intercessory prayer. The apostle Paul interceded for the Galatian Church because they had departed from sound doctrine, from miracles, signs and wonders and moved into legalism. The apostle Paul was basically saying *"I am in travail for you until I birth you"*. When you travail, things are birthed into the church, region and into the body of Christ. The Kingdom of God is birthed into existence (Isaiah 66:7-8).

2.   Groaning

This is a groaning that produces revival where there are no words spoken, only deep sounds and moans from deep within you (Romans 8:26). Paul spoke about this type of intercessory prayer where the Holy Spirit uses your mind, body and soul to release sounds too deep for words.

3.   Warfare Intercession

This type of warfare is where you war in another tongue. This type of intercession is so powerful that it breaks the curses and strongholds in the heavenlies such as Satanism, witchcraft, poverty and religious spirits. It is not birthing nor groaning, although this type of intercession may come with groaning sometimes. When warfare intercession takes place, you may experience an anointing come on you and manifest things like:

a.   Extreme aggressive militancy that comes on you.
b.   Physical demonstrations such as pointing with a finger to a particular place like a statue, tomb, business, house, heaven, earth; closed fists, jumping among others.
c.   Militant tongues and songs of the spirit.
d.   Prophetic acts and prophetic decrees like speaking things into the atmosphere.
e.   Identifying strongholds and curses, and speaking directly to them as if they were right there.

4.   Faith Intercession

In this type of intercession there is a supernatural release and activation of your faith, where the gift of faith works under the anointing of intercessory prayer. This type of intercession is used frequently in Prayer Level Two (Legal Battle) which we addressed in Chapter 2 of this book. It may manifest in various ways like:

a.   You boldly say things and make declarations of faith that that you did not plan on.
b.   You remind God of His promises. These are declarations of faith that are used to break the power of the enemy.
c.   You call the things that are not as though they were (Romans 14:7). There is a knowing deep within you which

cannot be explained that causes you to make decrees of faith with great conviction and boldness.

d.   You start to prophesy in an intercessory mode.

5.   Weeping

This type of intercessory prayer is not very prevalent in our day, but tears are very powerful. Washington Irving once said: *"There is sacredness in tears. They are not the mark of weakness, but of power. They speak more eloquently than ten thousand tongues. They are messengers of overwhelming grief, of deep contrition and of unspeakable love."* We need to pray and cry for our cities like Jesus cried over Jerusalem.

6.   Group Intercessory Prayer

It is good for intercessors to spend time praying in private. However, it is important to get together to pray in unity for a common objective. When this happens, sometimes there is a combination of birthing, travailing, groaning, weeping, and a high level of faith happening together in intercessory prayer where everyone is pushing toward the same place.

7.   Intercessory Prayer Team

The difference between an intercessory prayer group (IPG) and intercessory prayer team (IPT) is that the latter is a highly trained and disciplined team that prays continually every day, where they get into agreement and pray for something until they pray through.. It is extremely successful and effective and works closely with the spiritual leader of the house; whereas the (IPG) get together perhaps once a week to pray and intercede for the needs of the church and individual needs. We will address this in detail later.

C.   DIFFERENT TYPES OF INTERCESSORS

Whenever we get involved in intercession we need to cultivate a lifestyle of worship because intercessory prayer has a way of tearing down the body, whereas worship restores and rejuvenates the body. Every pastor should promote, stimulate, raise-up, train and mobilize intercessors in their local church. Jesus taught His disciples and trained them to do intercessory prayer. He gave them the story of the *'woman and unjust judge'* (Luke 18:1-8) and many other such illustrations (See Chapter 2). The key to the success of the Church in the book of Acts was intercessory prayer. That is why they were able to turn cities upside down. Intercessors are the key to bring about a breakthrough revival to our cities.

1. Natural Intercessors

These types of intercessors are anointed specifically for this ministry, and are the key to opening whole cities and nations to the gospel of Jesus Christ. Sometimes natural intercessors are able to change the course of whole nations as in the case of Moses, Abraham and Elijah. These are the ones whose natural calling and ministry is intercessory prayer. Natural intercessors are able to function in all levels of intercessory prayer.

Some people think they are intercessors because they intercede for a few minutes, but natural intercessors have a type of anointing that allows them to get into the spirit very quickly, and can pray and intercede for hours as the Holy Spirit possesses their whole being. When the Holy Spirit is calling you to intercession, the sign usually is a feeling of depression that comes upon you. Mature intercessors know that this means it is time to get alone with Papa.

Elijah was a natural intercessor who moved in the power of the Holy Spirit and changed the destiny of Israel. First he conducted *warfare intercession* on Mount Carmel against the four hundred and fifty prophets of Baal, as he made fire fall from heaven. Then he entered into *birthing intercession* as he prayed lying down on the side in a birthing position for seven consecutive times, until the rains came after three and a half years of drought. Then Elijah entered into the *groaning intercession* in the cave running away from Jezebel, as he received the command from God to anoint Jehu and Elisha.

2. Substitute Intercessors

These are the intercessors whose major gifting and calling is in another area, but from time to time the Holy Spirit pulls them into seasons of deep intercessory prayer. They can intercede in any of the seven forms of intercessions, and flow easily as they are accustomed to being used by the Holy Spirit.

These types of intercessors will feel the presence of God at a particular time leading them into a time of release as they are praying for specific things. When there are not any natural intercessors available, God will look for one of these substitute intercessors to use in intercession.

3. Temporary Intercessors

These are the intercessors that are used in seasonal times of intercessory prayer. When people that normally do not come out to prayer meetings start doing so, it is because the Lord is unlocking within their being a desire for intercession. These are people who never really pray and then all of a sudden the Holy Spirit comes on them and they begin to groan and moan.

Those who are mature intercessors need to show the other younger intercessors how to groan, travail and intercede in the Spirit. Like any other spiritual gift, intercessors have to be activated by an apostle, a prophet or another intercessor. If they do not see and hear others interceding, they will not intercede themselves.   There is a great need for all three types of intercessors in the body of Christ today.

D. THE INTERCESSORY PRAYER TEAM

Many churches have an intercessory group. However, an intercessory group that comes together to pray is not the same as an Intercessory Prayer Team (IPT). *'An Intercessory Prayer Team is a hard hitting spiritual swat team that is highly disciplined and trained to do intense intercessory prayer'*. The IPT can build a wall of fire around the pastor, spiritual leaders and church creating an *'open heaven'* over the city that will change the spiritual climate and prepare the land for an outpouring of the Holy Spirit. There is absolutely no excuse for not having an intercessory prayer ministry in the local church.

It would be beneficial to create three different groups of intercessory prayer gatherings in the local church. The first group is a basic one, and it would be open to anyone who would like to come and be a part of it. This group would serve to identify those who have the gift and desire for intercessory prayer, and recruit them as potential candidates to become a part of the Intercessory Prayer Team.

The second group is a bit more sophisticated and it serves to train those who have been identified and recruited as potential intercessors. In these meetings, mature intercessors would get along side the younger intercessors and show them how to do it. The third group is a more intense and specialized group made up of experienced and mature intercessors that we have termed the Intercessory Prayer Team. The IPT is a key, important element in conducting spiritual warfare.

Intercessory Prayer Teams build a wall of fire around the spiritual leaders, church, and city. It is strongly recommended for the pastor of the local church to be present during all the intercessory prayer meetings, but especially the IPT prayer gatherings. Some pastors do not want to get involved in this activity and delegate this task to a sister that has the gift of intercession as if it was something that was not masculine.

The absence of the pastor during intercessory prayer meetings has caused untold problems in the past. Sometimes intercessors become a problem in some churches by trying to exercise too much influence over the pastor and the church in general. However, in every one of these cases the pastor was absent during the meetings, and the intercessors had not been trained or taught properly. If the pastor wants to avoid having these types of problems, he must be an essential part of it. His mere presence will bring a balance to the group.

In order to insure the success of the IPT team, the spiritual leader of the house must not only be involved in the meetings, but must also have a close relationship and clear open lines of communication between him and all the intercessors. If the intercessors feel that their efforts are not being appreciated, failure will be inevitable. When a vital piece of information is passed on to the pastor by the IPT leader, he must get back to them with some sort of feedback within a reasonable time.

It does not matter whether his answer is yea, nay or not at this time, as long as he communicates his feelings and decision on the matter to the intercessors. The IPT leader should have access to the apostle/pastor during the week in order to be able to transmit whatever they have received from the Lord, if they are not able to do so during regular meetings. On the other hand, the pastor should be able to lean upon the IPT group for prayer support on ministerial or personal issues at any time.

Some people desire to be intercessors, but do not know how to do it and what is expected of them. Every pastor should dedicate time to the foundational teaching of such an important ministry, and periodically bring in an apostle/prophet who is connected to their church in order to train his people on these and many other key foundational topics. The pastoral anointing resting on pastors is adequate and good to pastor/teach the flock, but not to raise up five-fold ministries and intercessors.

Only apostles and prophets are equipped to do this type of training dealing with spiritual warfare (Ephesians 2:20-22). Apostles and prophets are set apart from the mother's womb, and throughout their lives suffer much rejection, opposition and affliction. It takes anywhere from fourteen to twenty four years to form an apostle/prophet. They are greatly needed in the body of Christ today and extremely valuable to the church in the area of spiritual warfare and intercessory prayer.

Apostles are endowed by God with great revelation, wisdom and apostolic authority to bring order into messy, stagnant situations. They flow in powerful miracles, signs and wonders as well as great wisdom and revelation. When a true apostle of God speaks, he has such an anointing on him that it causes a massive re-alignment in the hearts of men. He truly has a father's heart and thus is able to mentor without jealousy.

Prophets flow in a powerful anointing that breaks the yoke, births supernatural things in the spiritual realm and reveals deep hidden things. They have a unique ability to pull things from the realm of the spirit into the physical realm and manifest healings, signs and wonders with regularity. Prophets are natural intercessors who can easily get in the spirit and create breakthroughs in the heavens. They are the eyes of the body of Christ and precious in the eyes of the Lord.

1. Choose a Place and Time

Choose a time and place for the intercessors to come together and pray. This should be at least once a week, but preferably more often. This would be considered the place where the Intercessory Prayer Team comes together to do serious intercessory prayer.

The church is usually the best place to meet, but it could be held in another place appointed by the spiritual leader of the house. These IPT gatherings will be open only to members of the Intercessory Prayer Team.

2. Appoint an Intercessory Prayer Team (IPT) Leader

The Intercessory Prayer Team leader would be in charge of all the IPT meetings and become the focal point to which all prayer requests are brought to. The IPT leader could be a man or a woman, but must be a responsible, spiritual, trustworthy, wise and mature intercessor that has a clean Christian walk and a good testimony in the church and the community.

All the words of knowledge, wisdom, visions, dreams or prophetic words received in the homes, IPT gatherings or services should be brought to the IPT leader, who together with the other mature intercessors would then analyze them and decide whether to pray it into the heavenlies or bring it to the attention of the spiritual leader of the house for direction.

The IPT leader will be in charge of the intercessory prayer gatherings and will be submitted to the authority of the pastor or spiritual leader of the house. The IPT leader must have frequent meetings *(once a week is recommended)* with the apostle/pastor or spiritual leader of the house to:

a.   Report any dream, vision, prophetic revelation or words received during *(or outside)* the IPT gatherings.

b.   Receive confirmation, clarification and direction from the pastor concerning the steps to be taken, and strategies to be implemented.

E.   THE INTERCESSORY PRAYER TEAM STRATEGY

All new intercessors need to be trained through teaching, and by watching someone who is trained and experienced doing it. Every intercessor needs to be covered by another intercessor and by the IPT leader because demon spirits will come against them very strong. Many pastors have died because they did not have intercessors covering them in prayer.

Because intercessors walk so close to God and can hear the Lord so clearly, they may start to think that they have a greater measure of rule. But the ministry of intercessory prayer is not greater than the ministry of the apostle/pastor or the spiritual leader of the house, and all the intercessors must come into kingdom alignment and be submitted to him.

Praise and worship is essential to the intercessor for refreshing and strengthening of their beings. When you gather for intercessory prayer understand that there will be some demonic backlash. Do not let this discourage you, but instead prepare yourself and cover yourself with the blood of the Lamb. Find a covenant prayer partner that can cover you and be in unity with you.

Make sure you keep your life pure, separated unto God because this arena of the demonic and intercessory warfare is very dangerous. It is important that the intercessors be accountable to the IPT leader, and submit to the apostolic headship. The Intercessory Prayer Team should pray together to begin to soften the strongholds of the city by praying against them. They should target particular strongholds in certain streets and regions, coming against such things as strongholds of witchcraft, Satanism, drug trafficking, religious spirits, cults and others so as to break the strongholds of the enemy.

4

DIVINE STRATEGIES

"Spiritual Cartography"

A. HINDRANCES TO A MOVE OF GOD

The presence of God can only be brought into our midst if it is preceded by a season of preparation and sanctification. Many people seem to believe that inactivity means God is not doing much; however, sometimes the opposite is true. Joshua told the people to sanctify themselves before the presence of God would come to do wonders among them as they crossed over the Jordan (Joshua 3).

Just like the Israelites brought the Ark of the Covenant on their shoulders across the Jordan, likewise as New Testament priests and kings, we are to bring the presence of God on our shoulders to our cities. This speaks of intimacy with the Lord, and leads to divine authority and the right to issue divine decrees in His name.

Because of the many wounds the church has suffered through the years, wrong foundations were established, and have been there for a long time. These ungodly foundations must be rooted out, pulled out and destroyed, so that new godly ones can be brought in and put in place. For the presence of God to come into your city, some things need to take place.

1. Apathy and Lethargy Stifle a Move of God

The presence of God will not come into a city unless the people have an appetite for His presence. Do you really want the presence of God in your church, city, schools, in the streets, all around you everyday? Do you love the presence of God

45

more than your pastor, your church, your denomination, your pet doctrine, or your religion?

Christianity without the presence of God becomes just a religion. Unlike what many people believe, not every preached message from a pulpit is life giving and conducive to the presence of God. Dead religious preachers will preach dead sermons, and dead sermons will kill those who are willing to listen to it (2 Corinthians 3:6). These types of messages will breed doubt, unbelief and skepticism in the people, not faith.

2.   Prejudice and Racism Grieves the Spirit of God

As Christians you need to have such love and compassion for your city and community that you will not stop until you see a visitation from God. You cannot intercede for something unless you have gone through and are familiar with it yourself, because you will pray out of your mind, and not out of the conviction of the spirit. When the Church sees the city the way God sees it, the Church will change the way it acts.

We need to have a heart burden to want to see people treated properly and fairly, regardless of the color of their skin, ethnic group, background, education or financial status. This is what true justice and righteousness is all about. The Church needs to genuinely care about people, not just their souls. The people in turn will see the Church in a favorable light as the kingdom of God at work, and they will get interested.

3.   Religious Spirit Quenches the Presence of God

There needs to be a kingdom mentality or vision in the leadership of the local churches. There is no unity, love and trust among the believers, especially among the pastors and spiritual leaders of the cities. The people of God must start to genuinely love each other and treat each other right.

There is a reluctance in the local churches to work together in anything other than that which pertains to their own agenda, and will result in some type of benefit to their own churches or ministries. This type of wineskin, mindset and worldly structure cannot receive the outpouring of the Spirit God wants to send to your city. These religious paradigms and high places must be brought down before it can happen.

4.   Fear, Pride and Unbelief Hinders the Power of God

Most pastors are intimidated by intercessors because they can hear from God, while most pastors cannot. Their proud thinking goes something like this: *"Wait a minute; I am the one that is supposed to hear from God"*. Truth is all believers hear from God in different degrees. Every pastor needs to push pride aside, and humble himself and understand that certain people are naturally more gifted to hear from God than he is. Pastors should see intercessors as a gift from God to the local church, not as a problem.

Every local church should have an Intercessory Prayer Team (IPT), highly trained and disciplined in the art of intercessory prayer. All prophets are true intercessors, but not all intercessors are true prophets. True intercessors have sensitivity to the spirit realm that most people do not possess. True, genuine intercession that pleases God and achieves results will offend most people. This is because of ignorance and lack of teaching on the subject by most of the pastors.

Pastors do not trust prophetic people and intercessors in general. Even those pastors that seem to accept the ministry of intercessors in the local church have a problem keeping it running. Just like any car would have a problem in keeping its engine running if you do not put gas in it, likewise an intercessory prayer ministry needs to be kept running continually in order for it to be effective in the local church.

Breakdown occurs between pastors and intercessors because of fear, ignorance, distrust and lack of communication. When intercessors share something with the spiritual leaders, they need to listen and get back to them. A pastor must have a father's heart and understand the needs of the intercessors. He must cover them, nurture them, receive from them strategic information and give them feedback on it.

B.   SEEING THE CITY THROUGH THE EYES OF GOD

Do you love your city? Do you love your city with the love of God? You are not where you are by coincidence; God brought you there, placed you in that land and positioned you in that area for a specific purpose. That is the territory the Lord has given you authority over and your area of responsibility.

You have a commitment to that land. God wants to bring healing, reconciliation and revival to that city through you. Revival will come when the wall comes down between the church and the city. If you are going to see a transformation in your city, selfishness cannot be a part of your makeup.

You must determine in yourself that you will not leave your city until you see the fullness of God's presence, purpose and destiny manifested there. God is faithful. Whatever you sow into your city, the Lord will allow you to reap the results thereof. If you love your city, like any good farmer you must first start by clearing it of its garbage, and removing any defilement that prevents the presence of God from manifesting there before you sow the seed of the gospel.

The church has been called to manifest the kingdom of God on this earth, and that includes taking our cities by establishing the kingdom of God there. The problems that we see in the local church are representative of the problems in the city. These are problems that have never been addressed. At the heart of very city, there are spiritual roots that we cannot see, but yet we experience it every day in our lives.

The roots include you, people before you and the founders of the city. The natural is a reflection of the spiritual, and they are always interconnected. We need to learn how to remove the spiritual myopia that hinders us from seeing the city as God sees it. There is a very popular treatment today called Lasix, a laser surgery done by highly trained doctors where the cornea is reshaped, thus removing the impediment that causes myopia.

As intercessors, one of the main things you will be doing is removing those unnecessary impediments that hinder you from seeing what is really going on in the city. The Lord will allow you to start seeing things from a new perspective, and understand what is really happening around you. The church has been called to open the eyes of the people in the city; to bring revival to the city through repentance, reconciliation, redemption and restoration (Jeremiah 15:19).

Through intercessory warfare prayer the church will take back much territory for the Lord. As the people are turned from darkness to light and from the kingdom of Satan to the kingdom of God, they will be released into their destiny. As this begins to happen, the city will be positioned for whatever God wants to do there, and become whatever He ordained that city to be from the foundation of the earth, thus fulfilling its destiny and bringing glory to the Lord.

Unless we deal honestly and sincerely with the problems the local church faces, we will never have the power and authority to deal with the problems in the city. Many want to put problems under the carpet, pretending that they are not there. Prejudice, poverty, fornication, racism, religion, sin and the lack of power and presence of God in the church must be addressed before you can impact the city. Once you start to affect the spiritual fabric of the city, then change will come as God's presence once again comes and inhabits the land.

C. GENERATIONAL INHERITANCE

God is a generational God. Time after time He presents Himself as the God of Abraham, Isaac and Jacob (Genesis 18:18-19). When He sees a person, He not only sees the person, but his predecessors as well as his descendants; God sees a city the same way. People only see the problems in the city based on what they think those problems are, without understanding the root source of the problems in the city.

When you see a city the way God sees it, you start to see its historical roots, like who influenced it and how it was formed. Many times in the scriptures man is referred to as a tree. Every tree has branches, leaves and fruit that we can see. But everyone knows that no tree could exist if it did not have a root system to nourish it. We cannot see the roots because they are under the ground; however, we know they are there and they are responsible for the origin of that tree. Likewise, what you see today in a city is the fruit or the inheritance of past generations (Job 8:8-10; Exodus 20:5).

We have always thought that sin is an individual thing, but this is not always so. There is Biblical evidence of sins being committed by cities, even nations. In the book of Samuel we see a perfect example of how a sin committed by a ruler had national consequences for the following generation (2 Samuel 21:1). The cause of the famine was neither David's fault nor that of his people, but it was an inherited problem. Although Saul was dead, the people of Israel suffered the consequences of the sin that he had committed in the past.

You see, Saul in his zealousness to do the right thing for the people of Israel, had broken the covenant that Joshua and the nation of Israel had made with the Gibeonites, and although David had nothing to do with that, the nation of Israel was reaping the consequences of the corporate sin committed by his predecessor (Joshua 9:3-5;15,18). In this particular incident, the sin of one ruler (Saul) had consequences that affected a whole nation in the succeeding generation. The sin of Saul opened a door to the devil to bring famine into a whole nation although the sin had been committed by another ruler, in another generation.

These types of sins are referred to as corporate sins, and may also be done in the name of a culture such as carnivals, processions and pagan festivals. You are not able to see the sin, defilement, bloodshed, injustice and broken covenants that have taken place in the past, but you can see its effect on a city and start to recognize what a city really looks like to God, and can then begin to pray effectively.

Human beings were created in the image of God, and just like He is a triune God (Father, Son and Holy Spirit) we also are made up of three parts (body, soul and spirit) as taught by the apostle Paul in 1 Thessalonians 5:23. The body has to do with physical characteristics; the soul has to do with the mind *(intellect)*, emotions *(personality)* and will *(decision making)*; the spirit is the part that lets us communicate with God and perceives the spiritual realm (See Fig. 1)

Everyone knows that children inherit hereditary traits from their parents. These traits that are transmitted through our genes may be both good and bad. Some of these traits are tangible, while others are intangible and cannot be discerned as easily. In order to understand it better, we are going to break these hereditary traits into body, soul and spirit and look at each of these groups individually (See Fig. 2).

1.   Genetic Inheritance (Body)

We have all heard the expression at the birth of a newborn baby: *"He has the eyes of his father and the smile of his mom"*. The topic of genetic inheritance is familiar to most of us. It refers to physical traits and features that we inherit from our parents. Some of these traits may be good, while others may be bad. One child may inherit the athletic prowess of his dad, plus the good looks and mental acuity of his mom, while the other one might inherit the diabetes from the mom and the heart problems of the dad.

2.   Social Inheritance (Soul)

Children can inherit not only physical traits from their parents, but also intangible characteristics such as personality, temperament, culture, language and social conditions that will affect how they will look at life. We could call it social inheritance because it is the product of the social atmosphere where the child grew up and developed. If you take this concept and you apply it to people living in a city, you will begin to see the personality, culture and idiosyncrasy of that particular city start to take shape.

SCHEMATIC OF
HUMAN BEINGS

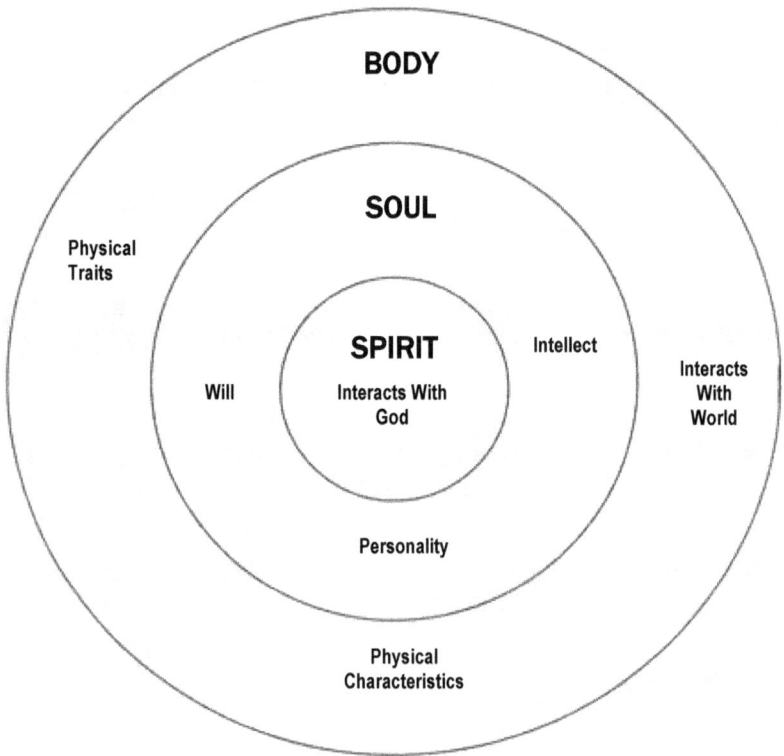

BODY

SOUL

Physical
Traits

SPIRIT

Intellect

Will

Interacts With
God

Interacts
With
World

Personality

Physical
Characteristics

Figure 1

SCHEMATIC OF POSSIBLE
GENERATIONAL INHERITANCES
IN HUMAN BEINGS

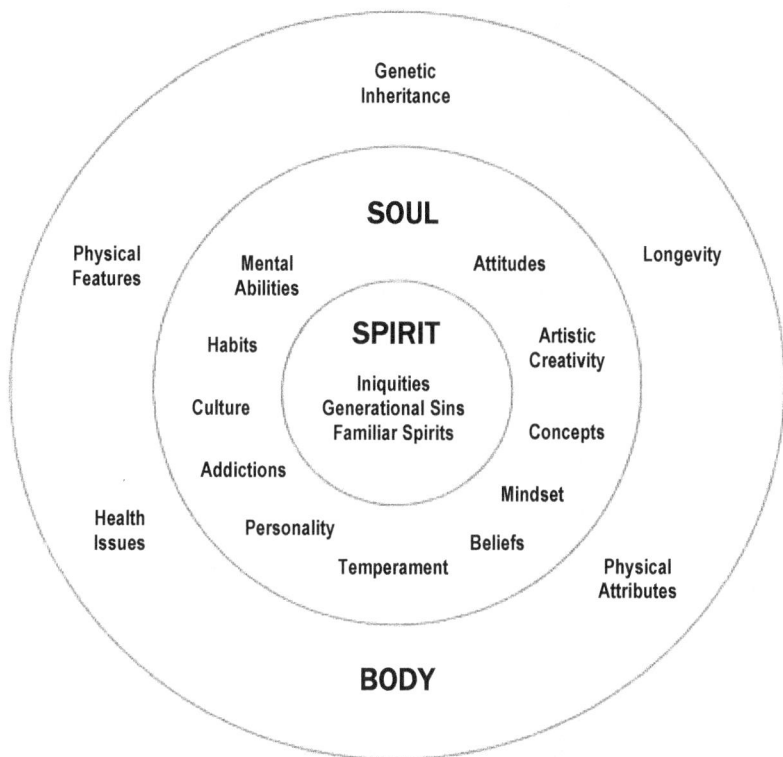

Genetic
Inheritance

SOUL

Physical
Features

Mental
Abilities

Attitudes

Longevity

SPIRIT

Habits

Artistic
Creativity

Iniquities
Generational Sins
Familiar Spirits

Culture

Concepts

Addictions

Mindset

Health
Issues

Personality

Beliefs

Temperament

Physical
Attributes

BODY

Figure 2

3.   Spiritual Inheritance (Spirit)

This part deals with the spiritual part that is passed on to a child that is not visible to human eyes and has to do with the sins of the fathers producing an iniquity or inclination towards the same type of sin in the children. Familiar spirits will try to make a person or family conform to their own traits or particular characteristic.

Unless the child is cleansed by the blood of the Lamb through the cross of Calvary, he will inherit the same spiritual weaknesses as the parents. Likewise, the spiritual iniquities of the people that lived in a land in past generations have now been passed on to the city.

Any church, business, family or person brought into the region will be influenced by the strongholds, bondages and mindsets of the area. After a while, they will begin to manifest the traits, characteristics, mindsets, habits and even the small mannerisms and idiosyncrasies exhibited by the majority of the people that live in the region

D.   THE SPIRITUAL ATMOSPHERE OVER A CITY

The church needs a paradigm shift in their thinking to understand that we are in a war zone. It must deal with issues that started many years ago which gave access to demonic strongholds and gave them territorial rights to influence the way people think and act in the church and city. There is an infrastructure in the demonic realm, just like there is an angelic realm (Colossians1:16).We know Satan is not omnipresent and omniscient so he needs and depends on many of his minions to carry out the war he is involved in.

Christ's victory on the cross must be applied and enforced through intercessory warfare in Jesus name; it is not automatic (2 Corinthians 10:3-5). The church has to do spiritual warfare to overcome the things that hinder the city from achieving its destiny. We are stewards of our land which is God's property, and wars are fought over land all the time. Land is always influenced by what people do while living on it. When the land where we live has been defiled, it affects the atmosphere in that region creating atmospheric pressure.

To heal the land, you must remove the original offenses and defilement that is affecting the city and causing the negative atmosphere in the region along with the physical consequences. It is the responsibility of the church to remove through intercessory prayer the things that are on the land that were never meant to be there. The kingdom of darkness usually tries to bring about the opposite of what the ordained will of God is for a region.

Every city has a character, which is composed of the traditions, cultures, religion, and mindsets of all the people who lived there from yesterday and today. These things help to shape and define the foundation of a city, and everything else is built upon it. There are strategic gates and doorways that must first be identified in the city, along with its demonic gatekeepers and doorkeepers before we can begin to do informed spiritual intercession and warfare (Jeremiah 1:9-10; 17-19). These gatekeepers and doorkeepers are demonically controlled people that have access to areas of influence within the city, and spheres of responsibility beyond the city.

A city where sin has never been addressed has a degree of guilt, shame, mistrust, economic failure, strongholds and people in bondage hiding from God. It also has other things such as idolatry, bloodshed, superstition, unforgiveness, secret societies, fornication, drugs, alcohol, legalism, occult activity, perversion, greed, jealousy, ambition and lust (not just sexual, but lust for power, control and authority).

In the book of Revelation, Jesus addresses seven churches and the problems each of them are experiencing telling them to overcome. The word 'overcome' is the Greek word 'nikao' and means to overcome, subdue, prevail, conquer and get the victory in spiritual warfare. If the church does not deal with its foundation and remove the issues that defile the land, whatever you build on the city whether it is a church, business or school, it will have the same root problems and issues of that land.

You may have heard the expression *'we are what we think'*. I am a firm believer in the validity of that statement; however, let me take it a few steps further. Whatever people in a particular city think about and ponder for any length of time, become their arguments or concepts which eventually develop into strongholds. Various strongholds together constitute a mindset or an ideology. Ideologies, mindsets and concepts influence the way people act. When people act and react the same way for a long time, it forms habits.

Habits that are practiced over a period of time usually are crystallized into traditions. Traditions eventually become a part of the culture of that city, which are eventually integrated into its society. This spiritual fabric will influence every single aspect of life in the city including the arts, education, economy, business, law enforcement, local government, and the church.

The repetitive, continuous action of people determines the spiritual atmosphere over an individual person, family, city or nation. It usually begins with a familiar spirit molding a person or family until they reflect the characteristics of that particular spirit. What began as a familiar spirit slowly becomes a generational spirit that eventually leads to a territorial power taking over the inhabitants of a city due to the acceptance of attitudes and conduct contrary to the laws of God.

The kingdom of darkness is nourished through the actions of people. That is why the majority of the people living in a city have striking similarities in their behavior. The actions of people in a particular place will determine whether the heavens are shut and the land is cursed, or the heavens are open and the land is blessed (Deuteronomy 28). This is how the covering of darkness is slowly formed over a city and nation due to the sins of its inhabitants (Isaiah 25:7).

The way people in an area think, molds their actions; these actions elevate certain spirits to a position of authority or rule over the area, bringing about a veil of darkness over the people of the city that hinders evangelism. Imagine the veil of darkness sin will produce over an area after generations of practice (See Figure 3). This topic of covering of darkness over

SCHEMATIC OF POSSIBLE
GENERATIONAL INHERITANCES
IN A CITY

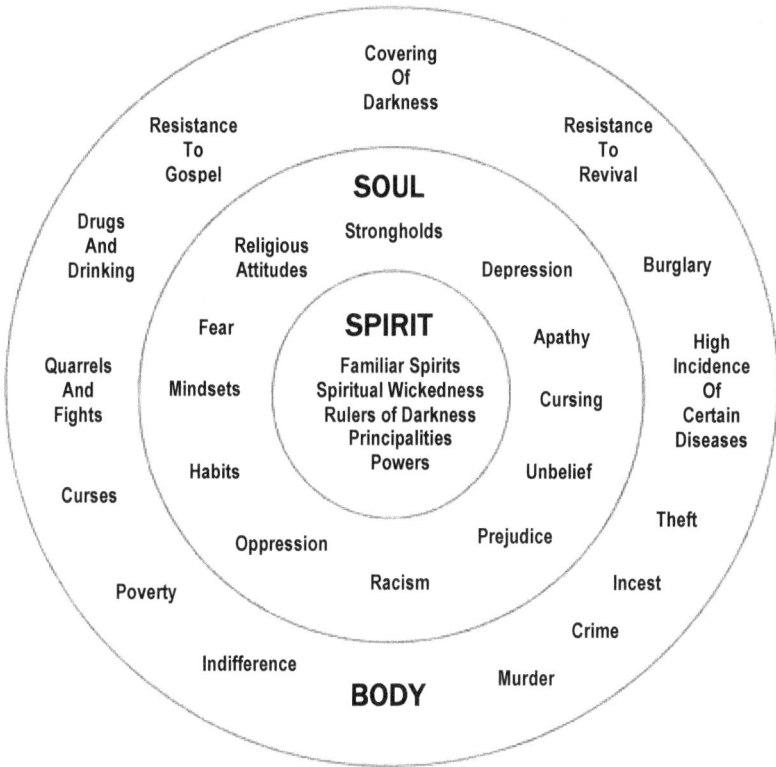

Covering
Of
Darkness

Resistance
To
Gospel

Resistance
To
Revival

SOUL

Drugs
And
Drinking

Religious
Attitudes

Strongholds

Depression

Burglary

Fear

SPIRIT

Apathy

High
Incidence
Of
Certain
Diseases

Quarrels
And
Fights

Mindsets

Familiar Spirits
Spiritual Wickedness
Rulers of Darkness
Principalities
Powers

Cursing

Habits

Unbelief

Curses

Theft

Oppression

Prejudice

Poverty

Racism

Incest

Crime

Indifference

BODY

Murder

Figure 3

57

an area is very important when it comes to evangelism. That is why it is necessary to remove this veil of darkness through intercessory prayer.

We must all understand the concept of open heavens and its effect on a successful evangelism and the harvesting of souls (John 1:51). The covering of darkness over an area plays an important role in the prayers of the saints being hindered as it was the case with Daniel; his prayer had been answered immediately, but the prince of Persia and the thick covering of darkness over that area hindered Gabriel the archangel from getting to him with the answer (Daniel 9, 10).

As I travel to certain cities, I have noticed that strongholds and certain things that are so evident to me are hidden to most of the people who live there. That is because the people that are under that covering of darkness are not conscious of all the problems, being themselves under that same darkness which alters the way they perceive reality (2 Corinthians 4:4, Job 37:19). We will now take a look at spiritual mapping and its role in removing the roots that were never a part of God's original intention or destiny for your city.

E. THE TOOL OF SPIRITUAL MAPPING

In Romans 1:19-21 the apostle Paul talks about the principle where we can discern the invisible things by the things that are made. If you look close enough, many of the natural physical characteristics and traits of a city will reveal the invisible spiritual forces and powers that gave birth to it originally. The root of a problem in a particular region coincides with the pacts and covenants the dwellers of the land made with the powers they worshipped.

You must understand that the physical realm is only a reflection of the spiritual. One of the main functions of the church is to remove every abomination and defilement that is stopping God's visitation from coming to and eventually inhabiting the city. No farmer would ever take his best seed and plant it in a land covered with weeds, rocks and debris and expect to receive a great harvest. The land may be good, but if it has never been plowed and cleansed it will not yield much of a harvest (Jeremiah 4:3).

Likewise, someone has to prepare the ground, unplug the ears and remove the blindfolds from the people that inhabit that land. In order to remove those issues and things that are an abomination in the eyes of the Lord, we must begin by looking for certain things in the city; some may be hidden while others may not. We see a biblical precedent for this in Numbers 13, when Moses sent spies to spy the land, and study the social, cultural and geographic aspects of the city of Jericho. They did their homework and so did the New Testament Church.

Spiritual mapping is one of the end-time revelations given to the church by God to see the spiritual condition of the world in which we live. It helps us to be able to see a city beyond our natural senses, and see it as God sees it. It is to the intercessor what an x-ray or an MRI is to a doctor, allowing him to make a better diagnosis, which leads to a more efficient treatment. It is a tool for intercessors to be able to do informed intercession (Proverbs 20:18).

Spiritual mapping helps us to obtain an image or picture of the spiritual situation in the heavenlies. It plays the same role that intelligence and espionage do in a real war, by revealing through the Holy Spirit the powers that operate in the spiritual realm over a territory, the strongholds in the city's cultural realm and its effect it has in the physical realm (Ecclesiastes 9:13-18). It is a spiritual, strategic powerful tool that reveals to the church the location and number of enemy strongholds and the most effective method to pull them down, therefore creating an open heaven over the city.

Once the church has a three dimensional map of a city, the intercessory prayer team will then be able to pray more specifically and effectively to open up the city for evangelism and have fewer casualties. Remember angels play a part as the heavenly warriors to aid the Church in defeating the enemy (Hebrews 1:14; Daniel 10:3; Psalm 91:11; Revelation 12:7).

Those involved will need to exercise extreme wisdom, tact and judgment. Do not divulge any information to outsiders who may show curiosity in what you are doing. Remember this is warfare, and the enemy will use anyone and anything he can to his advantage.

F.   THE NUTS AND BOLTS OF SPIRITUAL MAPPING

Just like human beings have a body, soul and spirit, likewise a city also has three parts (geographical, historical, and spiritual) that needs to be discerned in order to be able to pray effectively (See Figure 3). In order to be able to complete the spiritual cartography of a city, those involved will be broken up into three groups: geographical, historical and spiritual, with a specific task assigned to each group.

This will require much detailed, persistent hard work. All the members of each group must be sure to write down everything they see and hear. The Lord knows what issues in the city need to be addressed, and He will show and reveal the divine strategy necessary as you continue to work with Him.

The people involved may be intercessors, but do not have to be an intercessor or a part of the IPT team to participate. Each of these three groups must do their particular work separately so the process can remain pure, but should come together periodically to compare notes and receive strategic direction from the spiritual leadership. You will be surprised at how much everyone sees the same things. After a few weeks, the three groups will convene under the guidance of the apostle, pastor or the spiritual leader of the house to review their findings and develop a strategy for warfare.

1.   Historical Group

This group would be made up mostly of book worms and those who are computer literate since they will do most of their work in libraries, historical societies, chamber of commerce and also computer searches by surfing the web. They should get any information they can gather about notable events that took place in the past history of the city.

Remember that the Holy Spirit will be the one guiding you throughout this process, so you need to be very sensitive to His leading. The following lists of research topics and tasks are not meant to be exhaustive by any means, but only a beginning:

* The founders of the city and their dreams, purpose, religion, habits, landmarks, bridges, notable events, salient dominant features, names and traits of the area, businesses that predominate, anything out of the ordinary should be written down.

* Any relation between the native name of the city or its rivers to the personality and attitude of the inhabitants or anything that is related to the demonic or the occult.

* Any unusual characteristics of the city that distinguish it from others.

* Things that happen frequently such as homicides, suicides, violence, accidents, drownings and other tragedies that take place in the city.

* Places that are known by an event that took place there in the past.

* Anything that may suggest the presence of a curse or a territorial spirit.

* Any chilling story that took place in the past, including its cause and consequences.

* Make a list of who is who in the city's business world (past and present) and the family names of those that have been prominent in the city's political power structure.

* How and when did Christianity start in the city.

* The history of relationship among the races, religious conflicts and riots.

* Quantity of Christian Churches, few or many.

* Religious conflicts among competing religions, churches or Christians.

* Traumatic experiences such as economic collapse, earthquakes, hurricanes, etc.

* Names that have been used to label or describe the city and their meanings.

* Political, economic and religious institutions that have dominated the life of the city.

* The experience of immigrants or aliens in the city. How were they treated?

* The reason for the original settlement in the city, and its place in the national history.

* Wars that were fought in and affected the city.

* The leadership style of past governments.

* Historical data on the circumstances under which the gospel first entered the city.

* The religious practices of ancient peoples on the area.

* Historical data on the imposition of a new culture or language through conquest.

2. Geographical Group

a. This group would be made up mostly of energetic and dynamic people (young people would do great) who are more action and people oriented. These people need to be articulate and a wise judge of character who can extract information via social skills. Talk to the right people.

b. Get a map of the city (with streets shown) and place it where all can see it in the place of the IPT gatherings for reference and intercessory prayer.

c. After the group surveys the city, put down on the map anything they see that needs to be targeted by the IPT like: mosques, shrines and cults, bars, monuments, parks, idols, new age bookstores, satanic churches or witches covens, Christian churches, spiritual advisors, archeological sites, high violence and crime areas, and the socio-economical layout of the city. Look at the traffic systems, for usually it is symbolic of the spiritual reality of the city.

d.   Find out what movement Satan is using in the area, and who he is using. Talk to people who may know things.

e.   You can use different color pushpins representing different things, for example: purple-witchcraft, purple-free mason activity, yellow-homosexuality, black-hate groups (racial), green-gambling, red-violence, orange-cults like Muslims, Mormons etc. pink-new age activity, blue-pornography.

f.   Learn to be sensitive and led of the Spirit, and look at the city through His eyes.

g.   It would be good to take pictures or create drawings of things you see during your surveys. Take lots of notes.

h.   Keep a journal of where you go and what you did. Write down everything like weather, time strange occurrences.

3.   Spiritual Group (IPT)

a.   This spiritual group could be the most important of all because it reveals the reasons behind the symptoms discovered through the other two groups. It would be made up of the intercessors that flow in the gifts of discernment, and can hear God clearly.

b.   They would start doing intercessory prayer to receive revelation from the Lord about the spiritual strongholds of the area. They should write down everything they see and hear in the spirit, as well as any dreams they have. As reference material, I recommend to all the intercessors our book titled: *'Introduction to Signs and Wonders'*.

c.   There are some questions that the intercessors could ask themselves to guide them in their prayer time such as:

1. Are the heavens open in this place?

2. Is it easy to pray, or is there a lot of oppression?

3. Is there a discernible covering of darkness in the city?

4. Is there an area of the city more open than another?

5. Has the Lord has revealed to you the name of any principality, power or the strong man of the area?

d. The Lord may give you information in the forms of visions, words, names and pictures that together with the information received from the other two groups, would give you a complete picture as to what are the spiritual roots and strongholds of the city. Write everything down.

e. Once the IPT has information regarding these things, begin to pray for more clarity and precision as to the location and identity of the things the Spirit has revealed.

f. Remember this process may take a while, so exercise patience and persistence in order to receive all the information needed to begin the intercessory warfare.

g. The IPT need to cover each other, the spiritual leaders of the house, apostles and prophets connected with the house, as well as those who are on the front lines of battle.

h. The intercessors will continue to intercede and travail through this phase and into the next phase where the actual warfare will begin to take place.

Once the three groups have finished their investigative work and each group brings its information to the leadership, you will then have a spiritual map of the heavenlies over your area. Now you are ready to conduct informed spiritual warfare for your city under the direction of the Lord, displacing what the enemy has done and replacing it with God's destiny for that land through the ministry of intercessory warfare.

5

PRAYER LEVEL FOUR

"Spiritual Warfare"

A. GETTING STARTED

In Luke 11 Jesus went from casting out devils in verse 14 to the armed strong man in verse 21-22. This level of prayer is no longer casting demons out of people that are afflicted and oppressed, but it has to do with another level of prayer that deals with higher ranking demons assigned to families, churches, cities and nations.

We are not dealing with simple demons here oppressing the minds of people, but with the principalities, powers and the rulers of wickedness of the air, which require a much more intense and deeper intercessory warfare. They are not privates or sergeants in the devil's military hierarchy, but lieutenants and generals ruling over cities and nations.

Very few people ever enter into this level of spiritual warfare prayer, not because they cannot but because they do not understand it and have never been properly trained. Some have been taught by the pastors in some churches that they are not supposed to do such a thing, while others believe that they do not have the ability to do it. The truth of the matter is that you do have the power to engage the enemy and drive him out.

Start in your own home with things like strange pictures, statues, records, weird stuff handed down to you from unbelieving parents (especially those involved in the occult), gifts from your grandmother, uncle and even unsaved friends. Or maybe some strange looking decoration, doll, painting or any other souvenir that you bought in a foreign country and brought into your house. It may look normal, but somehow you have a strange feeling about it.

Why do people experience weird stuff that happens in their homes like lights going off for no reason, and doors shutting by themselves? I am not saying that there is a demon under every rock, or that you may have a demon just because you like to wear a red tie, have a tattoo or listen to some secular music. However, sometimes the Holy Spirit will reveal things that are so subtle that you do not notice.

The spiritual warfare battle for a city is generally headed by an apostle or a general of intercession. If a pastor or a Christian, no matter how anointed or how big a church he has, goes to conduct military battle and starts to bind the prince over the region without having first done the legal battle and won, he could be easily killed.

You cannot do spiritual warfare alone, especially in an area where you have not been sent. You must have won the legal battle (Chapter 2) and thus the right to wage war in that region. You need to be under cover; under the authority and in submission to someone who knows what he is doing, and has the spiritual authority to back it up like an apostle or prophet.

This is where you discover who the strong man of your city is. The strong man in a city or region could be a demonic prince, a governor, or Satan himself. He is the power demon assigned to a home, an area, city or country. This is where we enter the highest level of spiritual warfare. You do not cast out a principality or power from a city or a region; he can only be displaced through intercessory warfare and military battle.

Military battle is when you go to geographic places that have a history of intense demonic activity like witchcraft and satanic covens; places where much innocent blood has been shed and massacres took place; places where devils are hiding like abortion clinics, palm readers, sexual promiscuous places and curse them, commanding them to dry up and close in the name of Jesus. Now we are going to take a look at the spiritual doorways and gateways in your city.

B. SPIRITUAL DOORWAYS AND GATEWAYS

As the spiritual mapping of a city takes place, there are some things that you must be able to understand. You must dig into the heart of the city and see why the sin, decay and issues that brought the trauma to the area are there. You must find out how they entered into the landscape of your territory, and what acts were committed to trigger them.

There is a process to conduct intercessory warfare in your city. Before you sow your good seed in the land *(evangelize)*, like any good farmer there are some things you must do. First you must go out and remove the thorns, the stones and impediments *(sins and defilement of the land)*, by breaking away the bondages that have been created over time.

Once the bondages are broken, then you are able to take care of the birds *(evil spirits)* and keep them at bay *(binding and loosing)*, because evil spirits feed on bondages, and bondages feed on sin. Now you can start to check for rich soil there *(godly people and believers)*, and begin to sow the seed *(evangelism)*; this is how you do it.

1.   Demonic Doorways

Every city has doors and gateways that in times past gave Satan and his legion of demons access to enter into a territory. You must be able to discern these gateways and see them as God sees them; not in the natural, but in the spirit. These doors and gateways are opened in the spiritual realm every time certain acts are done by people inhabiting a land.

Whenever any of these acts are committed, it has a similar influence in five areas of the land: church, business, education, politics and society. You will see a striking similarity in the issues affecting each of these areas in a city. We are going to break down these acts into five areas of defilement: Idolatry, immorality, bloodshed, injustice and broken covenants.

These are the same five areas that King Josiah dealt with in 2 Kings 23, and after he dealt with these sins the land was restored quickly from famine, war, disease and ecological devastation. This is the process necessary for healing a land and making it whole, thus restoring it back to what the Lord had originally intended (2 Chronicles 7:14).

a. Idolatry

Acts of idolatry are done by people in the hopes of obtaining supernatural power. People enter into covenants with evil gods and come into bondages that can only be broken by the atoning blood of Jesus Christ. One of the most powerful gods today is Mammon, and has to do with money and material things. People controlled by the spirit of Mammon manifest a ruthless lust for power and control over others through manipulation and money. Individuality, initiative and creativity are discouraged and conformity and submission enforced.

b. Immorality

Acts of immorality are running rampant in the world today, but it is seen as normal by most people. The reason for this type of reasoning is that the moral standards established in the word of God are not seen as applicable to our present day society. Therefore, when there is no law to restrain humanity, you get lawlessness. Fornication, adultery, incest, child trafficking, pornography and other similar immoral acts have contaminated our land. These acts open up many doorways through which demons can now rule over cities and nations.

c. Bloodshed

There is something very powerful about the human blood. I do not understand it all, but I do know that the word of God says that life is in the blood, and He forbids men from eating it (Leviticus 17:11-12). There is definitely some type of connection between blood and the spiritual realm, and we see many references to it throughout the Bible, all the way from the book of Genesis through Revelation.

We see it in the Old Testament, when animal sacrifices were made in the tabernacle and its blood applied to the mercy seat in the Holy of Holies. We also see it in the New Testament, when the Lamb of God Jesus Christ shed His own blood on Calvary, thus opening a way for the sins of mankind to be cleansed. Satanists and witches know this and have frequently used blood sacrifices to open portals and gateways through which demonic spirits can come through.

God hates bloodshed of any sort, but especially when it is innocent blood. Premeditated murder and those committed through acts of rage, anger or jealousy contaminates a land and defiles it, bringing about a covering of darkness over an area that may last for generations. The Bible says that the blood of an innocent man speaks out from the earth (Mathew 23:34-36; Luke 11:50-51; Hebrews 11:4).

d. Injustice

When people commit unjust acts against one another, wounding each other through rejection and hurtful words, it brings a curse on the land by allowing entrance to demonic spirits. Words can heal, but they can also wound people causing traumas in life and many times separation from our heavenly Father. This type of wound breeds a spirit of rejection and guilt. It is terrible to be rejected by another human being, but it is even worse to be rejected by yourself.

Throughout history many atrocities have been committed in the name of religion, ideology, nationalism and racism. These acts become even more important when they are done by those who invoke the name of Jesus Christ. The scars of these acts still linger in many parts of the world like Europe, Africa, Middle East, Asia, South and Central America and yes North America. There are still many unhealed wounds in this nation.

The abominable human slave trades of Africa; the bloody Christian Crusades into the Middle East; the savage attacks and

69

conquest of Europe by the Moors; the brutal Inquisition by the Roman Catholic Church; the ruthless colonization by the Spaniards of South and Central America; the slavery of people of the black race and the oppression of the Indians in North America; and the Holocaust of Jews in Nazi Germany. All of these and so many others like it have filled the earth with injustice and contaminated many lands in the world to this day.

e.   Broken Covenants

We covered this topic in the Generational Inheritance Section of Chapter Four, and saw the consequences that broken covenants can have on the people living on a land. God takes covenants very seriously, being known as a God of covenants. Marriage is a covenant between two people, and the epidemic of divorces on the land will bring about a curse on its people affecting future generations. When the land is defiled with covenant breakers, it comes under the influence of the enemy.

As you come and stand in the gap, repenting for the sins of the past and renouncing the sins of the future, you dislodge the original sins and remove the foothold that the enemy has had on the territory. As you begin to deal with the sins of your forefathers, you need to destroy the roots of iniquity and bondages through the cross of Jesus Christ (1 John 3:8).

2.   Seven Gateways of the City

For the church to remove the wrong foundations and establish Godly foundations in the city, it needs to address certain areas in order to bring a sense of God's presence to the city, and be able to release His blessings. These blessings will impact the economy, creativity, innovation and security of the city through each of these seven gateways.

The church as a whole has had a closet mentality for too long. Every church in the city should try to be personally involved and build relationships with each of these areas if possible and cover them daily with much prayer.

a. Local Government

We all know how corrupt politics can be. All politicians that occupy a political office in the local government must be covered in prayer since they are in positions of power and authority, and thus responsible for passing and implementing laws in the local government.

The church must pray against corruption, greed, personal agendas and manipulation by various outside sources, and cover the politicians with prayer as much as possible.

b. Legal Department

The church must pray for every one of the people associated with the legal department like judges and lawyers and cover them with prayer because they exercise laws, and have been given authority over legal issues concerning the city.

Pray against corruption and control of judges and lawyers by outside sources who may seek to manipulate things for their own ends, and that justice is ministered with righteousness and equality for all, regardless of sex, race, money or social status.

c. Schools

The Church has committed a very serious mistake in going after the older generation, while ignoring the future generation. Much energy and planning goes into reaching and teaching the adults, while very little interest is placed in the children. It is much easier to impact the minds of children that have not been contaminated and are ready to receive the seed of the gospel, than it is to bring down and destroy strongholds and arguments in the minds of adults before teaching them the Word of God.

Every school must be covered in prayer including its superintendents, principals, students and teachers (especially Christian, godly teachers). Pray against violence, drugs and alcohol, especially in the day and age that we are living in. Children have sensitive, impressionable minds and the enemy would love nothing more than to fill them with lies and filth.

Also pray against groups with secret agendas such as the gays, witches, New Age, evolutionists and child molesters that they do not gain a foothold in your local School System. Try to become active, and visit the schools. Pray with the teachers, students, the Principal and try to build a relationship with them.

d. Newspapers and Media

All the local newspapers, editors and reporters should be covered with prayer as well as any media networks such as television and radio stations. Along with those mentioned before, this is a very high impact area that helps to mold the consciousness of the city.

Pray for unbiased and honest reporting of news and information, and find any believers that may work there and pray for them. Sometimes they may offer to allow the Church to share a word in a weekly column of the paper.

e. Police

The local police department and all policemen need to be covered with lots of prayer. They are involved day to day with maintaining law and order in the city, and are exposed to many dangerous life and death situations continually. Pray against corruption, greed and abuse of power in the police departments and policemen.

Offer to pray for the police department and the policemen. In some cases, the police department has solicited the help of the church in order to deal with a rise in crime in different parts of the world. This is something that should be happening in America, especially in the inner cities where crime is so high.

f. Businesses

Local businesses need to be covered with prayer because they are an integral part of the economic health of the city. The church must pray against a poverty mentality, and release a spirit of blessing and prosperity on the local businesses.

Lay hands on their buildings and prophesy to them. Every Christian Church should adopt a business to pray for and visit them regularly. Friendships will develop as a result of this and may lead to the salvation of many. Encourage the believers to launch out and start their own business all over the city.

g.   Hospitals and Doctors

Finally, all the health institutions and its personnel need to be covered in prayer. They are responsible for the lives and health of multitudes. Pray for the doctors, nurses, ambulances and emergency units for wisdom and discernment in diagnosis and treatments, and visit the sick and pray for them regularly.

C.   SPIRITUAL WARFARE

Spiritual mapping is not an end in itself, but only a tool to help us know what root problems we are dealing with in order to engage the enemy through spiritual warfare, which is also only a tool to achieve a complete victory through the means of effective evangelism.   Once the spiritual mapping of the city has been completed, the spiritual leadership of the house will convene with the teams to study its results, and come up with a strategic plan to conduct spiritual warfare and destroy the works of the devil (Hebrews 2:14).

During His ministry on the earth, Jesus dominated and was victorious over the enemy on three battle fronts. Likewise, today the church must be able to carry out warfare on these same three battle fronts at the same time: the spirit, soul and body (See Fig. 4). In order to carry out this three-pronged warfare effectively, a very efficient strategy that could be used is to have a group of people assigned to each front.

Each group would be highly trained, equipped and released to one of the three battle fronts. The prophetic intercessors would clear the airways by conducting warfare on their knees through the vehicle of intercessory prayer. They would also pray for anointing to be released on the preaching

THREE PRONGED
WARFARE

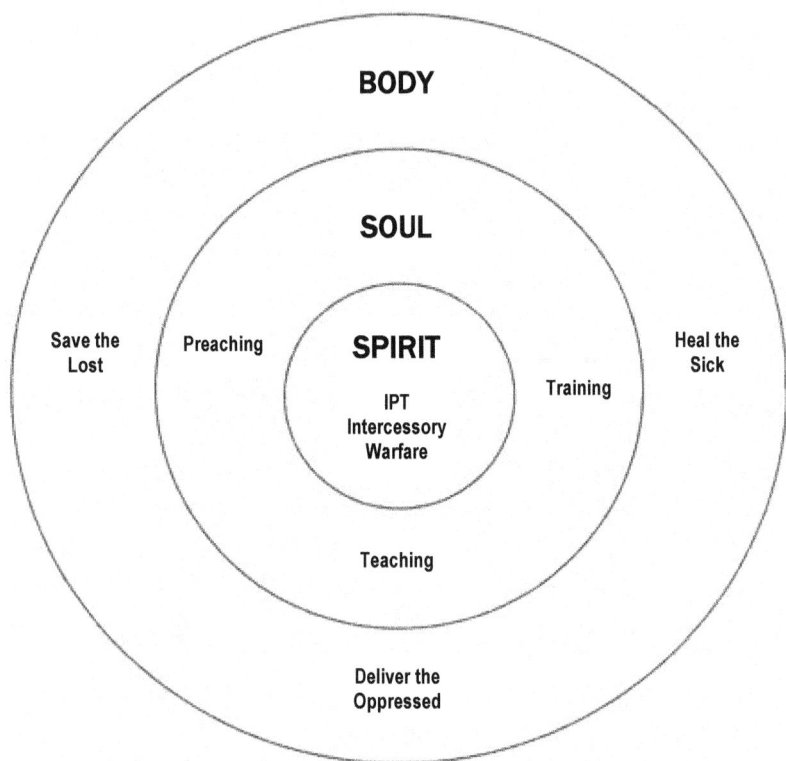

BODY

SOUL

Save the Lost	Preaching	**SPIRIT**	Training	Heal the Sick

IPT
Intercessory
Warfare

Teaching

Deliver the
Oppressed

Figure 4

of the word, and the people that will hear the spoken word of God. These prophetic intercessors would be a part of the IPT of the local church (2 Corinthians 4:18).

The apostolic ministers proclaim the gospel of Jesus Christ to the unsaved in the Church services, radio programs and street meetings. The message must be simple in content, and one that lifts up the name of Jesus and the power of His blood (Ephesians 3:10). The word is to be preached with passion and under the anointing of the Spirit.

Finally, a third group of evangelistic ministers would be in charge of reaping the harvest by ministering salvation, deliverance, healing and any other kind of need that may be present in those who receive salvation. This group would go out to the city and minister to the unsaved people there, wherever they can find them. This is the time when you must conduct aggressive evangelism.

Whenever you have open heavens over a city and revival is taking place, it is not uncommon to see over one hundred people being added to the church every week. A discipleship program must already be in place as massive numbers of people are going to be brought into the kingdom of God. Teachers and pastors must be prepared and ready to start teaching and shepherding the new converts.

1.   The Spiritual Realm (Airways)

This is where warfare is waged against the principalities and powers of darkness through intercessory warfare (Luke 10:19). This will involve prayer, fasting and intercession, but may also include prophetic acts, repentance and reconciliation.

This is a very important part of the battle. One of the first things that will happen when you engage your territory in spiritual warfare is the resident territorial spirit *(giant)* of the land will rise up against you to try to intimidate you and fill you with fear. In order to defeat and overcome these territorial spirits you will need to walk in humility, holiness and unity.

You must understand that demons do not have a body, so they cannot fight you physically. If they want to attack you, they must do it some other way. The only way these territorial spirits can affect and influence you is through your mind, or by using a vessel that is under their control.

In Matthew 18:18-19, Jesus gave His apostles the kingdom keys of authority to bind and loose. To bind means to prohibit, and to loose means to permit. Jesus told His apostles that whatever they declared prohibited on the earth would be prohibited in heaven, and what they declared permitted on the earth, would be permitted in heaven. The keys of the kingdom consist of the ability given to His apostles to permit or prohibit an action of spiritual nature on the earth.

Demonic princes must be displaced one at a time (Mark 3:26-27), and can only be defeated little by little and eventually dethroned by conducting intercessory warfare. True apostles submitted to Christ, working together with true godly prophets, have each been given spiritual jurisdiction and authority over specific areas to wage war and establish God's kingdom in that region, city, state and country (1 Cor. 12:28). After the victory, you may need to conduct clean up operations to deal with lingering demonic strongholds in the city (Mathew 12:29).

The strongman is usually a demonically anointed man or woman who is under the control of the ruling power of the territory. The scriptures do not say a strong demon or spirit; instead they mention a strongman (Luke 11:21-23). Before you engage the enemy and start removing defilement from the city, the strong man of the region must be discerned first, bound and overcome before you can plunder his house.

When the strongman in the city is identified, the lines of communication between him and the evil spirit that controls him must be disrupted so he is no longer under his control. Afterwards you must bind him, which is the legal term that declares that his activity has been prohibited on the earth. Once the strong man has been bound and overcome, you must continue to wage war against the enemy until you displace or push out every one of his generals and lieutenants that he has surrounded himself with in your particular city.

Keep in mind that the strong man is the main tap root of the enemy's control over a city, but not the only one. After this has been accomplished, you can then proceed to plunder his house. The IPT team must intercede for the salvation of the strong man if possible. Remember Jesus came to seek and to save that which was lost. He loves everyone, including that person that is used of the enemy.

If the person will not receive salvation, then the church needs to pray for the removal of this person from the area; one way or another. Once the person who had demonic spiritual authority over a city or region has been saved or bound, you will slowly begin to see the manifestation in the natural as the heavens open and the people are set free.

Teams are then set up to go out and prayer walk in the streets conducting warfare intercession in the areas where the strongholds are located, while another team stays behind interceding (Romans 16:20). This is the time when prophetic decrees and prophetic acts would be done under the leading and direction of the apostles and prophets and our Commander in Chief Jesus Christ.

Begin walking and claiming the streets for the Lord, laying hands on the businesses and buildings anointing them with oil as directed by the Holy Spirit, and releasing God's destiny for the land. Speak into the atmosphere and cleanse the airways (Col. 2:15). You will need to have perseverance and persistence in order to achieve complete and total victory.

2.   The Soulish Realm (Consciousness)

Whenever a territory is inhabited by people who have chosen to give their loyalties to the powers of darkness, that land becomes contaminated by territorial spirits that have been given a right to be there and keep the people bound, blind and oppressed. It will be necessary to first cleanse the land by identifying the enemy, and then engaging him in spiritual warfare until victory is won and the territory is redeemed (Ephesians 3:10; 6:10-18).

Once the church begins to declare the manifold wisdom of God over the city, coupled with the intercessory warfare being waged in the heavenlies by the intercessors, the principalities and powers will have to release their hold on the people that are being held captive in chains of bondage and darkness (Isaiah 45:2-3).

When the chosen anointed vessels of God commence to declare the Word, angels are activated and the enemy has no recourse but to flee. Whenever we decree the word of the Lord, we involve angels in the battle who hearken to the voice of His word and are quick to execute His will (Psalm 103:20).

The preaching of the word is how we take away the armor from the enemy. This is our fundamental weapon for the destruction of strongholds, structures, mindsets and paradigms in the minds of the people. The word of God is like a hammer breaking down every one of these arguments, thoughts and concepts that stand in the way of their salvation; it is like a sharp two edged sword piercing deep into the heart, separating their soul from their spirit (Hebrews 4:12), light from darkness and truth from lies and fables.

As the anointed vessels of God preach the unadulterated word of the Lord, the power of the Holy Spirit will rip the veils of blindness from the eyes of the people, allowing them to see the glory of the gospel of the kingdom. As the spirit of revelation comes upon them when they hear the word of the Lord preached under the anointing, the blindfolds will come off and the eyes of their understanding will be enlightened.

The preaching topics should be coordinated with the IPT, so that their intercession is in agreement with it. For example if the intercessors are praying against and binding the spirits of lust, fornication and adultery, the preaching should be on the topic of holiness and personal sanctification.

At the same time the local church should have deliverance, healing and counseling teams ready and available when the people start coming to the altar to receive salvation, healing, deliverance or any other need they may have. This is a very powerful strategy where the enemy is attacked on three fronts, and has been very successful in the past in foreign nations.

The last two verbs in Jeremiah 1:10 are to plant and build. This means that after tearing down and destroying the mindsets and paradigms which were opposed to the kingdom of God, the minds of the people need to be planted and built with the word of God. A psychiatrist or psychologist will tell you that the best way to get rid of a habit is to substitute it with something else.

3.   The Physical Realm (City)

The local church must get organized and build a proper infrastructure for effective evangelism, in order to fulfill the great commission, and the assimilation of new believers. You should keep in mind that this is the time when you plunder the house of the strong man and divide his spoils through aggressive evangelism. People will begin to receive salvation, healing, deliverance as the gospel is preached and demons cast out (Romans 1:16; 1 Corinthians 1:21).

The church has not acted with wisdom in regards to this topic. Generally most churches adopt the attitude that people will somehow find their way to the church, and there accept Jesus Christ as their savior. However, real evangelism is not a spontaneous thing. It is the fruit of well coordinated plans and efforts where the believers have been made conscious of their role as fishers of men (Mathew 4:19).

You need to keep in mind God's divine order for the church where every believer is called to the work of the ministry. The complete wineskin (the five-fold ministry) is called to perfect the saints by helping them to discover their talents, gifts and divine callings. They must then be trained, equipped and released to use their gifts and fulfill the calling on their lives (Ephesians 4:11-13).

To conduct strategic spiritual warfare and not follow it by aggressive evangelism is not something I would recommend. It is healthy to always remember that spiritual mapping is not an end in itself, but only a tool to conduct a successful spiritual warfare campaign. Likewise, we must keep in mind that all spiritual warfare is not an end in itself, but only a tool to prepare the territory in order to conduct effective evangelism.

Workers in the local church should be trained, and have their nets repaired and clean. By this time, the church must be prepared with evangelism materials and trained evangelists, who are ready to cast their nets and bring in the harvest of people who will then be assimilated into the kingdom of God. This is the time when you plunder the house of the strong man.

Pastors and teachers should also be prepared and ready to start teaching, discipling and pastoring the massive infusion of babies that are about to be brought into the kingdom. There is absolutely no excuse for a local church not to have an aggressive evangelism and discipleship program in place. There is much literature available today about cell groups, as well as discipleship courses that anyone can obtain.

Besides intercession, evangelism and discipleship, every church should have a strong ministry in three other areas: deliverance, healing and ministry to the needy. This is the pattern we see in the book of Acts New Testament Church, and in the ministry of Jesus Christ. The Lord not only preached the gospel, but ministered to the spiritual, emotional and physical needs of people by healing the sick, delivering the oppressed, feeding the hungry, and helping the widows and orphans.

Prophetic acts are also something that is done in this phase of the battle. Although prophetic acts deal with the spiritual, they are conducted on the physical realm. A prophetic act is an action done in response to a prophetic word such as the story of Elisha the prophet, and Joash the king of Israel in his battle against the king of Syria in 2 Kings 13:15-19.

Another example is found in Joshua 8:18 where the angel of the Lord told Joshua to extend his spear towards the city of Ai, for He had given it into his hand. Prophetic acts were done in the New Testament as well by Agabus the prophet (Acts 21:10-11), and even Jesus Himself such as turning the water to wine, and telling the blind man to wash in the pool of Siloam.

D. ONE LAST THING

Many of the cities and nations in the world that in times past were shaken and impacted by powerful revivals today lie in deep wickedness and evil vile corruption. If this teaches us anything, it is the fact that God has no grandchildren. It shows us that although it is possible to bring about open heavens to a city that produces revival, reformation and transformation, the hardest part really is maintaining what has been achieved.

If we could dissect every move of God, we would discover that it usually has four stages: breakthrough, revival, spiritual transformation and maintenance. Most churches will usually experience the breakthrough stage at one point or another. That is the stage where you begin to see some growth in the local church as attendance increases, and there is a feeling in the air that good things are about to happen.

The revival stage is when a local church experiences a supernatural flow of God's presence, and there is a high level of conviction, anticipation and great faith in all the services. Large numbers of people start getting saved, healed and delivered in all the meetings, and people cannot wait to be in the revival to experience the presence of God. Unfortunately, most moves of God stop at this stage.

The spiritual transformation stage is when the revival is not limited to the local church only, but it expands and starts to affect everything in the city. As it comes under the authority and power of God, the city also begins to experience revival. Bars and strip joints start closing down; crime rate goes down as the presence of God becomes real, and begins to permeate entire sections of the city and compel people to their knees.

What happens in each city will be different and unique to that particular region. Although some of the characteristics of revival are the same everywhere, God does not do the same thing in every place. Remember that each city is different, and we need to pray and find out what strategy the Lord has for each city. What happened in the Lakeland, Brownsville and Toronto revivals, may not be what God has for your city.

Once victory has been won and revival has broken out in your city you cannot rest in your laurels. We must borrow a page from the military handbook and learn how they do it once military victory has been achieved. If you look at the lessons learned in the Iraq and Afghanistan wars, you will see that the occupation phase of those countries was much more difficult to achieve than the actual military battle.

Once you have won the victory and revival breaks out in your city, you must enter into the maintenance phase. It takes great perseverance and determination to preserve the hard won victory over an area. When revival breaks out in a city, it will flow through and affect everything people do. There will be a paradigm shift in the way people think and conduct their daily lives, as the days of business as usual will be over.

It is very important that you understand that the enemy will fight fiercely to try to take back the land that he has lost to the kingdom of God. The attacks upon those that are occupying the territory he lost will be relentless and without mercy. Bear in mind that the enemy uses the guerilla type warfare of terrorism and intimidation. There are seven things that need to be done to protect and guard the city during this phase.

1. Intercede For the Leaders

The moment you engage the enemy of the land, the giants will appear. Goliath and his brothers will come to wage war against you. The pastor and the entire leadership team needs to be covered by the IPT, along with each member of the team. Prayer and fasting must be taught and practiced. Endeavor to always keep the lines of communication open among those in leadership in order to avoid misunderstandings and problems.

2. Fear God, Not Men

Whenever you engage the enemy of the city, he will try to put a spirit of fear on you to deter you from your goal. Remember he is a defeated foe and all he has going for him is intimidation and terrorism. Promote healthy, accountable relationships among leaders that promote unity, not jealousy.

3. Watch Against the Foothold of Sin

Whenever the enemy looses people in a territory, he will retaliate against you with great wrath. Be sure to be on guard against attacks from the enemy in the form of temptations and old habits wanting to get a foothold back in your life and all of the people involved, especially those in leadership and the IPT. Walk in love, purity and acts of kindness, not in legalism.

4. Guard All Foundation Areas

Once you lay down godly foundations, you need to keep them and guard them. It is important that local churches have apostolic and prophetic oversight. Someone who is trusted for his wisdom and insight should come frequently to make sure everything is running properly as well as to give new direction.

5. Teach and Establish Revival

Teach revival in the churches, schools and businesses wherever possible and whenever you can. Revival is a way of life, not something we have every so often. It must become a continuing, perpetual process in the lives of the people. The tangible presence of God needs to saturate not only every church service, but every activity in the life of God's people.

6. Establish Watchmen

There must be people who are continually in prayer, keeping watch and guarding the land. This is the main function of the prophets and intercessors. Every local church should have prophets and intercessors watching and guarding to make sure the enemy does not get a foothold in the church or the city.

7. Establish Gate Keepers

You must have a group of intercessors specifically praying for the seven gateways of the city. It is the responsibility of the local church to place the right people in positions of apostolic authority so they can release spheres of influence on the local church, land and the city. Go to the mayor and say: *'what can we do to help?'* This is how the kingdom of God is established.

E. CONCLUSION

This book is by no means a complete, thorough study on intercessory warfare and all the things that need to be done in order to take our cities back for God, but it is a good beginning. The legendary football coach Vince Lombardi once said: *"The quality of a person's life is in direct proportion to their commitment to excellence, regardless of their chosen field of endeavor."*

It is my most sincere prayer and hope that I have somehow challenged, motivated and inspired you to reach higher, think bigger and go further than ever before. May this book be a source of help and strength to you as you endeavor to create open heavens over your own life, home, church and city. I am going to leave you with a short excerpt from a poem of a notable man of God:

"Faith, mighty faith, the promise sees
And looks to God alone;
Laughs at impossibilities,
And cries it shall be done."

- Charles Wesley -

GLOSSARY OF TERMS

Activate To stir up and cause to come alive. Apostles and prophets have the ability to activate the gifts and callings of the believers that are lying dormant like the gifts of the Spirit.

Alignment To bring into agreement with God's perfect will by making an adjustment. When a church is out of order in some of its doctrines and ministries, it needs to be brought back into alignment by an apostle. The doctrines and ministries of the church must be aligned to God's word.

Apostle One who is *called out* and *sent* by God having divine authority to root out, pull down, throw down and destroy strongholds, paradigms and mindsets in specific areas through deliverance, healing, intercession, binding, loosing and preaching. They also train believers in foundational truths and kingdom order. In the Old Testament, prophets were the only ones called out and sent, but in the New Testament both prophets and apostles are sent. An apostle is a reformer whose character is one of humility, accountability, commitment, integrity and purity that is forged through spending years in the wilderness, alone with God.

Apostolic Reformation A term that is used by many today to describe the changes taking place in local church government in many parts of the world emphasizing the restoration of the apostles and prophets, as opposed to the more traditional denominational church structure and worldview.

Authority The lawful right to do what one has been sent or commissioned to do. It is the mark of apostles and prophets. Spiritual authority is recognized in the spirit realm by both angels and demons, and includes healing the sick and casting out demons. Without authority we cannot properly establish the kingdom of God.

Binding and Loosing Apostolic authority to restrain, forbid, stop or prohibit. To free, forgive, release, permit or allow something or someone. It started with the apostle Peter. It is not limited only to him, but also given to those who walk in revelation and apostolic authority.

Birthing To bring forth something or someone new. Apostles and prophets, with the help of intercessors birth new ministries, churches and movements (Gal 4:19).

Breakthrough A significant development that takes place when an obstacle that was hindering is suddenly miraculously removed or overcome. Apostolic ministry is a ministry of such breakthroughs. Apostles have a breakthrough anointing that helps to penetrate and overcome obstacles in their path that prevent the advancement of the gospel of the kingdom of God.

Casting Out Demons The act of casting out devils out of a person who is possessed or oppressed by them. Casting out demons is one of the characteristics of true apostolic ministry.

Cell Groups A principle of apostolic ministry based on the concept of small home groups and gatherings. The early church practiced this in the book of Acts when they met from house to house and also publicly.

Character Godly character and integrity are signs of a true apostle, along with supernatural signs and wonders and sound foundational doctrine (1 Thessalonians 2:10-12). Integrity in all things and dealings is apostolic and the plumb line against which all things are to be measured.

Church Growth It is the result of spiritual momentum that comes from intercessory prayer and anointed ministry. The early church in the book of Acts saw great growth as people were added to their numbers daily. When there are demonic powers and principalities in certain regions that are keeping the church from growing, apostles and prophets need to help breakthrough the barriers that hinder growth (Acts 8:14).

Church (Universal)   The body of Christ that is composed of all the believers worldwide. Every believer anywhere that is washed in the blood of the Lamb and calls on the name of the Lord Jesus Christ (Ephesians 4:4).

Church (Local)   The local gathering of a group of believers in a city or region to receive instruction or fellowship. Apostles and apostolic teams are instrumental in planting local churches in different cities.

Commission   To authorize; to give someone the legal right to function and execute a certain task. When God calls someone to be an apostle, He raises him up and gives him His anointing, power and authority. When the vessel is ready, he is then commissioned to do a specific work in the kingdom.

Confirmation   It is a spiritual authorization that establishes, confirms and gives credence to a word, ministry or a believer. Apostles and prophets bring divine confirmation to believers, ministries and churches. It usually comes through preaching, teaching or prophetic ministry, but it may come through other means such as dreams, visions or unusual occurrences.

Curses   A legal right given to demons to operate in the life of a person which can be identified through spiritual discernment, and broken in the name of the Lord Jesus Christ (Galatians 3:13). They could also be malicious, evil words spoken over someone or into the air. Some examples of curses are: premature death, chronic health problems, poverty, divorces, and certain diseases. The ability to minister deliverance and break curses is essential to apostolic and prophetic ministry.

Darkness (Covering)   One of the main functions of the apostle is to tear down the veil of darkness over a region, and turn the people from darkness to light. Darkness represents spiritual blindness, ignorance, satanic and occult activity, witchcraft and dark evil sinful deeds (Acts 26:18).

Decree   A divine, official, authoritative proclamation made by a believer or a person with authority. Apostles and prophets make decrees over people, churches, cities and even nations. A decree originates in heaven and then pulled down and released by one of God's chosen vessels. Decrees cause an alignment between heaven and earth to take place, thus releasing angels to accomplish the will of God on the earth.

Deliverance An apostolic ministry where demons are cast out of people. Jesus gave the twelve apostles power over the unclean spirits (Mathew 10). It is a sign that the kingdom of God has arrived. This ministry takes territory for the kingdom of God because demonic spirits are challenged and overcome through deliverance. Apostolic churches need to have a strong ministry of deliverance.

Demons Although the word used in the Bible is devils or evil spirits, they mean the same thing. Unclean spirits that come to oppress, harass and torment human beings. They must be cast out of people by believers who are living for God, filled with His Spirit and trained in deliverance ministry.

Destiny The predestined will of God. Apostles and prophets will help release God's destiny for a person, church, city or nation. The preaching of an apostle releases a sense of destiny.

Discipleship The training and equipping of believers in the Christian faith. Apostles do much training and equipping in the church. Pastors and teachers do teaching, but the apostles train believers and release an impartation upon them that strengthens them and helps them to achieve their destiny.

Equipping The training and furnishing of the saints. The five fold ministry was given to equip the believers to do the work of Jesus through apostolic ministry. Apostles and others of the five fold ministry will equip through preaching, impartation, teaching and activation.

Gatekeeper A porter or one who guards access to a place or city. A symbol of authority. Apostles and prophets are the gatekeepers for cities, regions and territories. When there are no gatekeepers in a city, it opens the door for demonic spirits and evil to come in like a flood.

Gateways/Doorways Represents access and authority. The elders and rulers sat at the gates in past times. Principalities and powers seek to control the gateways and doors to a city to establish satanic strongholds there and prevent the kingdom of God from succeeding in that city. The gates of the city were restored by Nehemiah, who is a type of the apostolic ministry.

Giants Strongholds of darkness that attempt to occupy the land through intimidation and giving believers a grasshopper mentality. Driving out the principalities, powers and high ranking demons from a region requires intercessory warfare.

Gnosticism A false teaching that emphasizes knowledge and philosophy. It was the greatest threat to the early church that the apostle Paul warned about (Colossians 2:8).

Heaven (open) A spiritual climate in a region that is conducive to salvation, healing, miracles, deliverance, financial blessings, breakthroughs, worship, church growth and liberty in the spirit. We can see this in Elijah the prophet's ability to open the heavens. Apostolic churches must operate under open heavens.

Heaven (closed) A spiritual atmosphere that is heavy and sometimes oppressive, that hinders the operation of the Holy Spirit. There is a lack of salvation, miracles, healings, blessings and spiritual breakthroughs. Apostles and prophets have the grace and authority to open the heavens and bring on a release of the outpouring rains of the Holy Spirit.

Holiness A life of purity, righteousness and pursuit of God. The ministries of apostles and prophets help to bring standards of righteousness and holiness to the church. When these two ministries are not operating in the church, it opens the door to all kinds of worldliness and carnality.

Humility One of the essential characteristics God looks for in a person and necessary for everyone in ministry, especially for apostles. Early apostles walked in humility and brokenness. They were neither driven by personal ambition nor sought any personal titles or offices for themselves.

Impartation Laying on of hands on a person for the purpose of imparting some gift or grace, although it can also be done by the preaching of the word and prophecy (1 Timothy 4:14). The apostles laid hands on believers for the purpose of receiving the Holy Spirit (Acts 8:18). Moses also laid hands on Joshua to impart to him the gift of wisdom (Deuteronomy 34:9).

Integrity The ability to do what is morally pure and righteous in your life, time after time without fail. A quality of life that brings a person into alignment to the kingdom of God. The main quality missing from the character of false apostles and prophets, and evident in the life of the real ones.

Jezebel The un-submissive wife of Ahab, who in scripture represents manipulation, intimidation, deceit, rebellion and control. One of the main ruling principalities in America, especially in the church. This spirit vehemently opposes and persecutes the ministry of apostles and prophets because of their authority and power in the kingdom of God.

Judgment The ability to be able to discern or perceive critical or difficult situations and make reasonable wise decisions. An essential part of apostolic ministry in the governing of the local church, as well as dealing with rebellious, difficult people.

Kairos A Greek word that is used to describe the appointed time God has ordained for something to take place on the earth (Acts 17:26; Galatians 4:2, 4).

Kingdom of God God's sovereign rule and reign over His creation. The domain where the King reigns and governs with righteousness, peace and joy in the Holy Ghost (Romans 14:17). Manifested with power and authority through signs and wonders like casting out of devils, healing of the sick and other miraculous events (Mathew 10:7-8).

Laying on of Hands One of the foundational principles of the Christian faith as outlined in Hebrews 6. It is done for impartation, healing, deliverance, receiving the Holy Spirit, prophecy, ordination, promoting and releasing ministries. Paul the apostle warns against suddenly laying hands on a person either for ministry or promotion (1 Timothy 5:22).

Legalism A strict adherence to the letter of the law in the present Christian dispensation of grace; placing more emphasis on the outward form and ritualism than on character, substance and spontaneity of the Spirit by any church or group of Christians. It brings people into bondage, not spiritual liberty.

Love The most important quality in the life of a Christian, and the main commandment that was left to us by our Lord Jesus Christ (1 John 4:7-11; Mathew 22:39-40). It is unselfish, loyal and compassionate towards other people, and fulfills the law according to Romans 13:10.

Mandate A specific authoritative command, instruction or an order given by God to one of His servants. A heavenly vision or directive given to a chosen vessel for the purpose of advancing the kingdom of God on the earth, in spite of severe persecution, obstacles or enemy opposition.

Mantle The invisible covering that rests upon a person symbolizing the anointing, power and authority of the apostolic or prophetic office. A mantle is earned through a life of faith, service, obedience and dedication. There is always a price to pay to receive a mantle, as was the case with Elisha receiving Elijah's mantle (2 Kings 2).

Martyr One who chooses death rather than renounce his faith in the Lord Jesus Christ. One who sacrifices something which is very dear or important to him out of obedience to the Lord in order to further the kingdom of God. Someone who endures great pain and suffering. True apostles and prophets are marked for martyrdom the minute they are born in this world, and mostly live a life of persecution, pain and suffering.

Mentor The name of Odysseus' wise, trusted counselor and adviser. A mentor is much more than a coach or teacher, it is someone who takes you under his wing like a father to train, nourish and protect you. A mentor not only teaches you, but imparts to you part of his spirit and character.

Molech   One of the main principalities ruling over America today, who in the Old Testament demanded the innocent blood of children. Today it manifests in the form of abortions and in Satanism, witchcraft, sorcery and the occult (Leviticus 18:21).

Mountain   An obstacle that stands in the way. A demon that is assigned to hinder and delay God's plan and will for your life. Apostles have the grace and faith to overcome and remove the obstacles that the enemy brings to hinder the advancement of the kingdom of God in a life, church or region.

Mysticism   A spiritual discipline that attempts to have spiritual mystical encounters with the divine through meditation and superstitious self-delusion, beyond the ordinary understanding of the Christian faith. It has always been a problem for the Church, and is not to be confused with the divine revelation of God's mysteries given to apostles and prophets.

Occult   Pertaining or dealing with any supernatural phenomena beyond the realm of human comprehension. This includes but is not limited to witchcraft, Satanism, astrology, palm reading, necromancy and divination, which is all forbidden by the Bible (Deuteronomy 18:10-12). When there is occult involvement, it opens the door to demonic activity and requires deliverance.

Open Door   Refers to having access to go to a certain place, as opposed to closed doors, which means the lack of access or entrance into a certain region or nation (1 Corinthian 16:9).

Open the Eyes   Refers to the eyes of understanding in people being opened so that they can receive the gospel of Jesus Christ (Acts 26:18). Only intercessory warfare has the ability to rip the veil from the eyes of people. The ministry of apostles and prophets also has the ability to open the eyes of understanding in people because of the strong prophetic anointing and revelation which is present when they minister.

Order   A condition where all things are in its proper place, healthy and doing exactly what they should. One of the main functions of the apostolic ministry is to bring revelation, restoration, healing and order to the body of Christ thus establishing the kingdom of God. The devil operates in a state of confusion, lawlessness, oppression and chaotic disorder.

Paradigm A structure, wineskin, pattern or set way of thinking developed through the years. It takes apostolic ministry to break and tear down those structures, strongholds and pastoral paradigms in the minds of people, and replace them with an apostolic mindset, strategy and function. As long as the church has a pastoral mindset, it will never reach outward to the cities and nations, and the people will never reach their potential.

Paradigm Shift A change in the structure, pattern, mindset or set way of thinking. A shift is taking place right now that will usher the church into the apostolic reformation. This will not do away with pastoral ministry, only enhance it. The way the church operates right now is not able to contain what God wants to do. The present paradigms in the church do not allow apostles and prophets to operate properly, and the people to function in their gifts and callings as they should. The church needs an apostolic structure in order to utilize all the gifts, power and revelation the Lord is releasing upon the church.

Pastor One who shepherds a flock by feeding it and taking care of it. This ministry is being redefined with the arrival of the apostolic reformation. Many pastors are truly apostles that are operating under a pastoral anointing because they have very limited understanding of apostolic ministry, and have never been trained or released into it. The ministry of the apostle also involves shepherding people, but has many other pastors operating under his covering in the house.

Pattern A plan, a diagram or model to be followed in making something. The Christian Church must be built according to the heavenly pattern given to the apostle Paul by revelation from the Lord Jesus Christ (Ephesians 2:20-22; 4:11-16), just like the tabernacle of Moses had to be built according to the heavenly pattern given to Moses by God. The present pattern that most churches are using is faulty and needs to be replaced.

Peace The absence of hostilities, disagreements, quarrels and war; harmonious relations. Apostles have the grace to be able to release peace into the atmosphere of the local church, where there has been confusion, division and strife. In all his letters, the apostle Paul greets the churches by releasing peace to them (Romans 1:7; 1 Corinthians 1:3; Galatians 1:3; 1 Timothy 1:2).

Persecution The constant oppression, harassment, affliction and distress of human beings, sometimes to the point of death, especially for reasons of their belief. Apostles and prophets suffer much persecution throughout their lives because they preach and say things that are misunderstood and rejected by so many Christians of their time. Every restoration movement has experienced rejection and persecution at some point.

Power Evangelism An evangelism style that uses the gifts of the Holy Spirit to win the lost. Phillip used signs, wonders and miracles to start to evangelize Samaria (Acts 8:5-7).

Principality A demonic prince ruling over a territory to expand the kingdom of darkness, and keep the Church from advancing.

Prophet One who speaks by divine inspiration and through whom God reveals His will. Some prophets are seers, others are dreamers, but they all have the ability to see into the future. Prophets along with apostles are foundational ministries given to the church. There are many who have prophetic anointings in their lives, but not many walk and operate in the office of a prophet. Not all who move in the gifts of prophecy and words of knowledge are prophets. The making of a prophet involves years of forming and training alone in the desert.

Prophetic Intercession A type of intercessory prayer that is prophetic. Because intercession is the main function of a prophetic ministry, all true prophets are prophetic intercessors, but not all prophetic intercessors are prophets (Amos 3:9).

Pulling Down Strongholds One of the main functions of the apostolic and prophetic ministry. Apostles have the grace, anointing and supernatural ability to demolish mindsets and mental structures that have the people bound in religion.

Reformation To form again something that is defective, by removing, improving, changing or correcting the errors or defects. The great Protestant Reformation of Martin Luther is a very good example. The reformers always move in an apostolic anointing at specific, appointed times.

Release To set free from confinement, restraint or bondage. It is not enough to teach, equip and train the saints, they must be released into their callings, and given the authority to operate in it. Apostles have the grace, wisdom and authority to release believers to fulfill their callings without feeling threatened or intimidated by their particular giftings, talents and anointing. A pastoral mindset is too restrictive and fearful of releasing believers, which stunts their growth and development.

Resistance To work against, fight, and actively oppose the gospel of the kingdom. Principalities and powers over a region do this by working through the people in the land, sometimes causing persecution to come on the believers.

Revival Times of refreshing and renewal where the Lord visits His church, strengthening believers and bringing a harvest of souls into the kingdom. True revivals like the ones at Azusa and Whales impacted and transformed cities, not just churches. Recent revivals like the ones in Toronto, Pensacola and Lakeland have impacted only the local church, leaving the cities untouched. There have also been some carnal excesses and demonic manifestations in the meetings that have turned many people off. All these things do not mean that the revival was not from God, but only that He used imperfect, human vessels that are ignorant of these things.

Rooted A believer that has been discipled and grounded in the foundational principles of Christianity, so as not to be tossed to and fro by every wind of doctrine (Colossians 2:7). Every born again believer needs to be rooted and grounded in their faith.

Root Out To dig up things that are rooted deep in the ground of the hearts and minds of people. Apostolic ministry has the ability and authority to root out strongholds and wickedness that is imbedded deep in the consciousness of people through warfare intercession and apostolic preaching. Planting of good seed can then start to take place, thus building the kingdom.

Saints Born again believers, who according to the Bible have been redeemed and washed by the blood of the Lamb. Those who have decided to live a life of purity and surrender to their Lord and Savior Jesus Christ.

Salt A white substance used to preserve meat and give flavor to foods. Used to stop corruption both in the natural and the spiritual sense. In the Bible Christians are referred to as the salt of the earth, preserving it against immorality, evil and corruption (Mathew 513).

Snakes and scorpions Types of unclean evil spirits. Every believer has the power to cast out evil spirits, but training in deliverance is recommended to avoid excesses and harm to all parties involved. Everyone who is sent should operate in the ministry of deliverance and healing, which are apostolic traits.

Servant One who serves in submission, performs certain duties and promotes the interests of someone else. All believers should have a servant's heart, but especially those in positions of leadership and the five fold ministry. The word minister means '*to serve*'. The higher a ministry, the more of a servant's heart he should have.

Shepherd One who pastors, guards, feeds, protects, and cares for the sheep. Not all shepherds are apostles, but all apostles are shepherds. Shepherds sincerely love the sheep and will give their lives for them. Shepherds love to be with the sheep, and likewise. They seem to have an anointing that attracts sheep and makes them feel comfortable and at peace in his presence.

Signs and Wonders God has always used supernatural signs and wonders to distinguish and authenticate those who are sent (Mathew 10:7-8; 2 Corinthians 12:12). Paul cites the chief traits of an apostle's ministry to be supernatural signs, wonders and miracles (Romans 15:19). The gospel of the kingdom is not complete without signs and wonders being manifested.

Strong man The term used to refer to the principality or ruling demon over an area that keeps people in bondage and hinders the gospel from advancing. The strong man must be identified first and then bound in order to take away his bounty (souls). The ministries of apostles and prophets are necessary in order to overcome these ruling spirits (Luke 11:22).

Team ministry An apostolic concept where different people with diverse giftings are grouped together in order to achieve a common goal for the kingdom of God (Acts 13:1-4; 15:40-41). Jesus sent out the seventy disciples two by two (Luke 10:1). Some examples of team ministry are the intercessory prayer team (IPT), the counseling and ministry team (CMT), the healing and deliverance team (HDT) and the prophetic and apostolic team (PAT).

Territorial spirits High ranking demonic princes and ruling spirits that have been given access and control over a specific nation, area, region, city or neighborhood by its inhabitants and thus have a legal right to be there. These types of spirits cannot be cast out, but must be displaced through intercessory warfare and apostolic ministry.

Traditions A set of unwritten cultural customs, thoughts or behavior done by people from generation to generation in a particular nation, region, area or city. When traditions are placed above the word of God, it creates serious problems and leads to hypocrisy in the Christian lifestyle (Mathew 15:6-9). Although all traditions are not bad, some of them are, and need to be examined in the light of God's word.

Transition The process of changing from one form, state, place or activity to another. The world goes through times of transition and so does the church. Transitions are painful but necessary. Throughout the centuries, the Christian church has gone through several times of transition as it moved into more revelation from the word of God. Starting with the Protestant Reformation, we have seen the church go through many transitions and movements, as it makes its way to its original condition. We are presently in the final transition that will usher us into what has been termed the *Apostolic Reformation.*

Unclean spirits Demonic spirits, devils, evil spirits all mean the same thing. The word unclean is used because of the corruption, evil and contamination associated with evil spirits. These unclean spirits defile and contaminate human beings and whatever they inhabit be it human, animal or a place.

Unity The state, quality or condition of being in agreement. The fundamental agreement of interdependent and different people or components producing harmony of thought and purpose. The prayer the Lord Jesus prayed in the Garden of Gethsemane (John 17). One of the qualities of apostles is to promote unity in the body where there are differing callings, gifts and talents. The anointing only flows through unity.

Vision A supernatural event initiated by God where a person sees into the spiritual realm things that occurred in the past, present or future. When dealing with past or present events it is functioning together with the spiritual gift of the word of knowledge. When the vision deals with a future event, it functions with the spiritual gift of the word of wisdom or the prophetic. Apostles and prophets usually flow in visions and dreams, but any believer can receive a vision from God.

Warfare The waging of war against the kingdom of darkness. Warfare is going on all the time whether you realize it or not. You have already been involved in some type of warfare, you just did not realize what was going on. There are three levels of warfare conducted in Christianity (2 Corinthians 10:3-6).

Warfare (Level One) The first one is the lowest level and it has to do with the personal temptations, battles and warfare that every believer deals with in his daily life (1 Timothy 6:12). As long as we are on this earth, we will have to fight the good fight of faith in our daily lives.

Warfare (Level Two) The second level deals with the ministry of healing/deliverance where devils, demons or unclean spirits are cast out of people and homes are cleansed (Mathew 10:8;

Mark 16:17). New converts or believers that are not walking close to the Lord and living pure lives should not attempt to be involved in this type of ministry. Anyone who has a desire to be involved in this type of ministry should receive prior training from someone who has had extensive experience in the ministry of deliverance.

Warfare (Level Three)   The third level is the most intense heaviest type of warfare and it deals with waging battle against principalities, powers, rulers of wickedness in high places and high ranking territorial spirits over a region (Ephesians 6:12). Apostles and prophets together with the intercessors are usually the ones mostly involved in the second and third level of warfare by nature of their calling and ministry. The agents of Satan involved in the occult, sorcery, witchcraft, Satanism, divination and other areas are dealt with in this level of warfare (Acts 8:9-24; 13:8-11; 16:16-18; 19:18-20).

Watchmen   Those who are responsible for warning the people of any approaching danger. Usually the prophets or seers were the ones that acted as watchmen in the land of Israel. Today this role is given to prophetic intercessors to guard and protect apostolic churches from demonic attacks and ravening wolves.

Weapons of warfare   Usually refers to the ministry of spiritual warfare and intercessory prayer. The saints cannot defeat the enemy and the kingdom of darkness by using carnal weapons, or human worldly wisdom. Our weapons are spiritual, and we must learn how to use them with wisdom in order to overcome the strongholds of the enemy and be victorious in battle.

Wells   Types of the refreshing waters of the Holy Spirit. It is sometimes used to describe a place where the presence of God flowed at one time in the past. The enemy plugged the wells of Israel in order to weaken and destroy them (Genesis 26:15-18). Just like Isaac had to re-dig the plugged wells his father Abraham had dug, today we must do the same to bring back the flow of living waters where it has ceased. Water is very important to maintain life in the natural, as well as in the spirit.

Wineskin Symbolic in the Bible of mindsets, methods and structures in the church. An old wineskin represents legalistic, traditional, inflexible, ritualistic and rigid styles of ministry that were formed during an old outpouring or move of the Holy Spirit in years past. Jesus told the Pharisees that old wineskins could not contain the new wine that He wanted to pour into them because they would break. New wineskins represent the paradigms, revelation, structures and methods that are released during a reformation. Apostles come to renew old wineskins or create new ones that are able to receive the outpouring of the new wine that God wants to give.

Wisdom Understanding of what is true, right or lasting. Keen perception, sagacity, sound judgment or good common sense. Apostles are wise master builders known for their godly wisdom and their ability to impart sound judgment into a difficult situation. Jesus told His apostles to be wise as serpents and gentle as doves (Mathew 10:16). Apostles have the grace and ability to release the peace of God to the Church.

Witchcraft Black magic, divination or sorcery. Identified in the Bible with the sin of rebellion, legalism and the works of the flesh (1 Samuel 15:23; Galatians 3:1; 5:20). The spirit of Witchcraft must be broken through intercessory warfare.

Wolves Represents any type of false ministry that comes to devour, harm or take advantage of the sheep (Mathew 7:15-18; Acts 20:29). Watchmen and shepherds watch for wolves making sure they do not get close to the sheep. There are not only false prophets in the church, but also false apostles, false pastors and false teachers referred to in the word of God. Jesus said that by their fruits you would know them (Mathew 7:16).

Works of the flesh (dead works) Carnal, lifeless, formal works that are based on greed and selfish motivation *(rather than on obedient acts of faith)* which shall not be rewarded by the Lord, but instead will be burned during the Judgment Seat of Christ (Galatians 5:19-21; 1 Corinthians 3:10-15).

www.ingramcontent.com/pod-product-compliance
Lightning Source LLC
Chambersburg PA
CBHW071820020426
42331CB00007B/1565